CALL ME MOSES

CALL ME MOSES

BY J. MOSES HARPER

Edited by Damon C. Sugameli

Photos by Alicia Newkirk

CALL ME MOSES
Published by J. Harper, New York 10452
Edited by Damon C. Sugameli
Photos by Alicia Newkirk

GOD

*Thank YOU for allowing me to be inspired
and encouraged.*

Special thanks to:

Alicia Newkirk

Michiyo Ishikawa

Mira Gandy

*Without you ladies, I wouldn't have been able to do
this.*

This book is dedicated to:

*E. Randolph Harper, Michael Jackson, R. "Shugie"
Windham,*

and my students.

"The biggest mistakes I've made took place when my intentions and my actions were out of alignment. My best memories were moments when doing what was in my heart to do produced amazing results..." – Moses Harper

GOD   LORD
LOVE   PEACE

I was just thinking to myself, that if I write my life story it might hurt some people's feelings, though it is not my intention. To the contrary, I believe in acknowledging truth because as harsh as truth might be at times, healing resides within it. Lies don't have a strong foundation, being that they lack a real starting point. You can't move forward if you never even began. Having said all this, it's pretty safe to assume that when you encounter me, whatever you see, that is my truth. You might not like it—some days I don't even like it—but it's reality. As you read, please keep in mind that my perspectives have gone through a healthy evolution over the years, and many of the negative feelings I had are no longer part of my psyche. While my outlook has matured, the actual events and details that took place I will not dispute, however I've chosen to omit the names of some individuals to protect their privacy. I'd also like to warn anyone who thinks they're about to read a fairytale that this is no such thing. I was forced to relive many disturbing events in order to accurately tell my story. This could not be accomplished without taking long pauses in-between writing, in order to recover, and I'm sure that had I not, writing this book could have killed me.

If you've already made up your mind to judge me, please do yourself and me a favor: stop reading. You don't really want to hear what I have to say, and I don't want to waste my time talking to a wall. As for everyone else, thank you for taking a moment out of your precious existence to get a glimpse at little, insignificant, me. I hope my story inspires you to bring out the best in yourself so that your life can be as happy as possible.

- CHAPTER 1 -

Fade into Existence

When you ask someone about their earliest memories, it's typical that these first recollections took place when they were within the age range of a toddler. For me, I remember myself lying on my back in a large bed. It was as if I were waking up, though I hadn't been asleep. The only way I can describe what I experienced is to say that I slowly faded into the awareness of my own existence, and I was afraid. What was I afraid of? Now I refer to her as Janice, my biological mother. I don't know exactly how old I was, all I can tell you is that I could not yet walk. I started walking when I was nine months old. You do the math.

During this first memory, I made a note to myself that I needed to try my best to keep track of what was going on around me so that I'd know what to expect. This decision was made on pure instinct, and it allowed me to retain things during my infancy that I wish I could forget.

Janice was violent and verbally abusive towards me, and my sister Cheryl who's 11 months older than I am. Anything could set Janice off, which would result in her beating us, so I would try to be as still as possible so as not to gain her attention. Sometimes I would sit in an uncomfortable position for long periods of time hoping that she'd forget that I was even there. When my father was home, Janice seemed to dilute her brutal nature towards us, which put me a little more at ease. It took me a while to figure out who he was, but I felt better when I realized that he seemed to hold as high of a rank over me as Janice did. Unfortunately my father was out during most of the day, so even when he was around, I proceeded with caution in fear that I would pay for it later when he left the apartment.

There are plenty of instances where I recall Janice's cruelty, some of which stand out more than others. Once she served me a bowl of Rice Krispies that was drenched in sour milk. I was still in a high chair and could not yet articulate that there was something wrong with the milk other than saying, "Milk is bad." She insisted that I couldn't come down from the high chair until I'd eaten all of it. Dad wasn't there for me to flag down and get a second opinion, so I was stuck. When Janice left the room, I used the washcloth that she'd left to put a fresh coat of cereal and spoiled milk on my tabletop. I was trying to make it look like I was cleaning up a mess that I'd made. When Janice came back and saw what I'd done, she beat the shit out of me. My father returned home soon after and Janice reported my crime to him. When I told him the milk was bad, he took a sip from the carton and poured it out immediately, confirming that I was telling the truth. Strangely, some part of me was expecting Janice to apologize. She never did.

My fear of her occupied my mind constantly. She used to beat us to make us clean our room faster. Her belt buckle would leave bloody cuts on my legs and knees that I thought would never heal. That was just plain ridiculous. Flailing down hard enough to draw blood from a couple of toddlers to make them work. Sometimes she'd hold me dangerously close over boiling pots on the stove and threaten to cook me. She often punished us without cause by sending us to bed in the middle of the day. We would just lie there quietly for hours until she'd walk by our door on her way to the bathroom and ask why we were in bed. We'd respond, "You told us to go to bed." To which she'd innocently reply, "Y'all can get up now." Her reactions to anything reminding her of our presence, regardless of whether or not it was offensive, were inconsistent. I'd often wonder if her reign over me was permanent.

I eventually figured out a tactic that occasionally saved me from a beating. All things came to a halt if I had to use the bathroom. I potty trained rather early, as I didn't like the feeling of sitting in my own mess. I'm sure Janice must have appreciated this detail about my rapid development, being that it meant less work for her. That being said, if I had to go, it was made a priority. I decided to use this pattern against her. Janice would put me on her lap and just as she was about to strike, I'd say, "I gotta go to the bathroom." My guess is she probably figured I'd lose control of my bladder—or bowels—during the beating. At this point, she'd tell me to go to the bathroom, but ordered me to come right back. I knew that she intended to commence the beating once I returned, so I did the only sensible thing I could come up with. I sat on the toilet and strained, pretending to egest, until she remembered that her "stories", (soap operas), were on and returned to her room to watch them. At that point, I would quietly step down from the throne and go back into my room, hoping she wouldn't remember.

I have to credit GOD for my level of understanding of what was going on in my surroundings, because to be quite honest, no one taught me a lot of the things that I'd figured out. For instance, I knew what a gun was for, but I had enough sense to know not to fire one. One evening, I came across my father's .38 on his coffee table. I was curious about its weight but I knew Dad wouldn't dare let me pick it up for fear that I might make a habit of it. I was quiet when I took hold of it and felt its weight, which ended up being as heavy as I had estimated it would feel. Within a few seconds, I put it right back down as I had found it.

My formal education about drugs and alcohol didn't start until I was much older, but somehow I knew that Janice was always drunk. She literally reeked of alcohol. Maybe the fact that she was a heroin addict and alcoholic, who drank at least two quarts of liquor a day while pregnant with me, had something to do with my instincts about the subject. I was later told that when I was born, I smelled like I had been bathed in alcohol. Dad and Janice often argued about the bottles of what I learned to call "wine," which she'd hide between our box spring and mattress. After a heated argument, sometimes she would sleep in the bed with Cheryl and me. I hated this arrangement because being around her gave me the creeps. It was a good alternative for her because she could drink her liquor in peace. One time she spent the night in our room and I woke up feeling a pain in my leg from what I thought was her leg draped over mine, which was typical. I lay there crying quietly hoping she would change her position, not wanting to stir her. When I couldn't take the pain anymore, I peeked under the covers to assess if I could free myself without detection. When I discovered that it was my sister's leg, I abruptly pushed it off, feeling like a damn fool.

My sister hated me, but I wasn't afraid of her. She would call me ugly or stupid, or just say bad things about me in general, but I never returned her insults. If she were having a calm moment, we would play until she grew tired of me. Having her for a sister was like having a friend who treats you like crap but you deal with it so that you're not completely alone. My relationship with her made me sad, but with Janice it was different. I had no bond with her. All I felt towards her was a deeply rooted fear that would stay with me well into my teens.

Thinking back on what a nervous wreck I was back then still frustrates me. Not because of my experience in particular but because the situation still exists for so many children. Being afraid is the catalyst behind hatred, violence, prejudice, jealousy and anger. Too many children start out life knowing fear, which results in them making horrible choices and following destructive patterns while relating to the world. I guess you can say my motivation to try to "save" people began during my early years, when I so desperately wanted to be rescued from my own turmoil.

I had no idea that the deterioration of Dad's relationship with Janice would mark the beginning of what would end up being one of the worst periods of my childhood. As I stated earlier, they often argued about Janice's drinking, but one day I overheard a very heated dispute that sounded like it was turning violent. My father never hit Janice, nor did he beat us, so hearing physical ruckus between them was quite alarming. Honestly speaking, even during their arguments, Janice was really the one doing most of the yelling. Cheryl and I were trying to make out what was being said when all of a sudden, Janice called for my sister. Cheryl went to see what Janice wanted while I nervously waited in our room. I could hear Janice barking something at Cheryl and apparently Cheryl's reply or reaction was making Janice even more furious. My father was calmly talking to Cheryl and soon she re-entered our room looking worried. She said Janice was trying to make her hit Dad. It was only a matter of time before Janice was calling for me. As I left our room, I was hoping with all my might that Janice wouldn't tell me to do the same thing. They were in the bathroom and when I looked inside, I understood why Cheryl was so troubled about what she'd seen. Janice was trying to attack my father and he had her pinned over the toilet. He was trying to talk her down while holding her wrists and using his weight to keep her from bucking. Being 6'4" and 200 pounds of lean muscle, my father could have easily killed her with his bare hands but all he did was restrain her. Janice began ordering me to go into the kitchen and get a butcher knife to stab him or a cast iron pan to "…knock the shit outtah this muthafucka!" She was screaming and looking at me with a level of intensity that didn't make me wonder for a second about whether or not she was joking. In a reassuring tone, Dad was telling me to go back into my room, but I suspect that he saw the hesitation in my eyes. Janice saw it too because she barked louder, commanding me to do as she'd said. I hesitated, not because I was thinking of doing it, but because I didn't know whether to defy Janice to her face or to turn my back on her while she was shouting at me. I didn't know which act of defiance would warrant me the more severe punishment. I just stood there crying, knowing that I was done for because there was no way in hell I could carry out her order. Hurt my father? Was she crazy? I finally went back into my room, still quite upset. My sister was analyzing what was being said during the heated exchange as it continued. Janice apparently had it in her mind that I was on her side but she couldn't have been more wrong. I tried to voice my frustration stating, "I don't like Daddy and Mommy fighting!" This outburst was a huge mistake. As soon as Cheryl heard my statement, she took the first half of it, "I don't like Daddy…" and ran into the bathroom to tell my father that I said I didn't like him. It was all Janice needed to confirm her hypothesis. My father marched into our room moments later, looked me square in the face and shouted, "You don't love me no more, I don't love you no more!" I tried to explain but I was so upset that I couldn't get the words out fast enough, nor could I match his volume. As he stormed back out, Cheryl returned, triumphant that she was now his favorite and Janice followed behind Dad to gloat. I collapsed into sobs feeling like my world was officially over. All of Janice's beatings combined didn't hurt me as badly as I felt when my father said he didn't love me anymore. Dad was the only one I wanted to be around. I loved him with all my heart. I could live without the other two. They didn't like me anyway. I could see the hurt in his eyes as he shouted at me. It must have broken his heart to hear that ugly lie my sister told him. It's one thing to be attacked by a person whose actions and rhetoric are routinely irrational. It's another thing to find out that your child, whom you've never done wrong to, has made up her mind that she doesn't like you. He never looked at me quite the same again. Years later I couldn't help but think that the reason he didn't take as much interest in me was because deep down he felt I didn't really like him.

If I had to make an educated guess, chances are this wasn't the first time Janice tried to make him believe that Cheryl and I had an allegiance to her over him. When it got to the point that she was trying to hurt him physically and could possibly get at least one of his children to join in, it didn't make sense for him to keep trying to make things work with her so that we could all be a family. Shortly after this episode they split up, and Janice took us with her to live in her cousin's apartment.

- CHAPTER 2 -

To Live A Nightmare

The day we left my father's home is a day I will most likely take to my grave. I didn't know that this was going to be the last time I'd see my father for quite a while. I remember Janice getting us ready to leave, when my father questioned whether she'd bothered to feed us yet. She was trying to argue that we weren't even hungry but Dad insisted that she feed us before we leave. I was hungry but I wasn't about to ask her to feed me. She once kicked Cheryl in her back, knocking her to the floor as they left my grandmother's home, because Cheryl asked for something to eat.

Cheryl and I were seated in the foyer, waiting to leave, when Janice came in with a bag of groceries she'd dropped. A glass jar of grape jelly had broken inside the bag, but that didn't stop Janice. Drunk as all hell, she started pulling shards of glass out of it so she could make us a couple of tired-looking peanut butter and jelly sandwiches. The image of a drunk, half-hearted woman scooping out jelly laced with booby traps to feed her young is still shocking to me, and I was there. I remember thinking that I'd have to eat carefully. Knowing Janice, she'd most certainly miss some of the shards of glass and I didn't want to cut myself. I couldn't allude to any of this, of course. In addition to the sandwiches, she scooped black-eyed peas and rice into an empty Wonder Bread bag with a large serving spoon. Soon after that, we were off to her cousin's place.

Janice's cousin, whom I will refer to as Big C, was more like a sister to her. Big C and her husband were also drug addicts/alcoholics. They lived in a housing project in the South Bronx, in a 2-bedroom apartment with their three children: Mitch who was around 7 years old, followed by Yvonne who was 4, and lastly Ron who was roughly a year and a half. Cheryl and Yvonne were only a few months apart in age and Ron was the only one younger than I was.

The memories of living in that place are so horrific that I had to "come up for air" occasionally, as I recalled them to write this book. The first night we were there began on a fair note, but it wasn't long before I got a glimpse of what it meant to live in a nightmare. All of the kids were in one of the bedrooms while

Janice and Big C watched television, smoked weed and drank in the other bedroom. There was a small table in the room we were in and my cousins had been told not to play around it because it had a shaky leg. I stepped out of the room for a minute but when I returned, the table had fallen over. In the end, Cheryl and Yvonne were the ones that Janice and Big C blamed for it. The punishment that they received could have easily earned the two women 10 years in prison. They lowered Cheryl and Yvonne out of the window with ropes as if they were going to drop them. After this, they stripped the girls down to their underwear and tied them to the heating pipe and a radiator stationed in the corner of the room. I was in a state of disbelief. Was it possible that someone could do this to a child and honestly be referred to as their "mother?" My sister had ill feelings for me, but she didn't deserve this and neither did my cousin. I hated seeing them being tortured like that. It didn't matter if they had knocked the table down. Even if it was on purpose, there was no excuse for such a savage punishment. I promised myself that if we ever made it out of this, I wouldn't let anyone hurt Cheryl like that again. The image of her crying and looking so helpless haunted me for years. As I was watching what was taking place, part of me suspected that Janice took the punishment to an extreme because Cheryl reminded her of Dad whom, to my knowledge, Janice hated. I made a mental note that I would be extra careful not to cross Janice in this place, not knowing that I was in no way prepared for the horrors to come.

That night we were sent to bed without dinner, something that Dad would not have allowed. In fact, I only remember eating one meal that wasn't scavenged while we were in that residence. The three "adults" only came into the apartment to sleep or party with their friends. They didn't cook for us, so Cheryl and I joined our cousins looking for scraps from the takeout that the adults left behind. We'd eat dried pasta or scrape up the dried spots of food and crumbs from the stove and pans that they'd cooked their meals in. There were plenty of cans of food but we couldn't get any of them open. If we were lucky, my oldest cousin Mitch would sneak slices of bread and make us all mayonnaise sandwiches. Getting caught stealing food was an automatic beating and I'm grateful to this day that my cousin was willing to risk it in order to feed us. There was also a neighbor whom everyone called "Shorty" that would visit often. He would always happen to have a big bowl of something he'd cooked with him. He'd ask if we could have a little taste and made a point to feed each of us. It was never confirmed, but I'm almost positive that Shorty's visits had almost nothing to do with fraternizing with the adults in the house. I believe he came there to help us.

The first night in that place was one of two occasions where I could remember being fully clothed while living there.

Walking around in our underwear was our typical look. Even back then, that seemed fucking disgusting to me. I hated being in filth. My aunt used to tell me how I would try to change my own diaper as an infant. She said I would have succeeded in doing so if I had figured out how to fasten a fresh one. During the time we spent in that residence, I only recall two baths, one of which I initiated resulting in me getting beaten by Janice for making an attempt to clean myself. The other in which she washed my hair with Tide powdered laundry detergent to treat the bugs that eventually infested my scalp. This set my scalp and eyes ablaze. Soapy water still soaked my hair as she sent me out into the living room to dance for some man she introduced as my new father. I just stood there, cold, naked and crying with a musty towel on my shoulders and that damned Tide burning the hell out of the back of my head. The guy tried to shake my little hand and make small talk, but he didn't seem very impressed with what was going on. I never saw him again.

With Yvonne around, Cheryl basically forgot I ever existed; not that she paid much attention to me anyway other than to say something harsh. The best part about living there was that I didn't have to see Janice every day. Sometimes we wouldn't see an adult in the house for a few days. When Janice came in with her friends, she'd make me dance and drink "Night Train" or "Thunderbird" to amuse them. She said it was cough medicine and

seeing how I had developed a terrible cough that lingered, I figured
she was trying to be helpful for once. I couldn't understand why
those drunken losers would start laughing every time I took a sip
from the bottle until Cheryl told me. Cheryl had been sent back to
the room for failing to swallow her alcohol properly. When Janice
was done with me, I found Cheryl in the bathroom hacking up the
liquid and trying to wash her mouth out. She saw me and said,
"Don't drink it, it's bad. It's wine. It's not cough medicine, she
lied." At this point, knowing what it was did me no good as I was
expected to drink a lot. I couldn't store the liquid in my mouth and
spitting it on the floor was a waste of liquor, which was out of the
question. I only had two options: do as I was told, or get beaten. I
did as I was told. The liquor burned my throat and I would either
feel disoriented soon after or just fall asleep. As bad as it sounds,
those were my first performances: dancing and drinking alcohol
for a bunch of fuck-ups. Janice also made it a habit to send me to
light her cigarettes on an open flame from the stove. I learned on
my own how to do this carefully without burning up the cigarette
or my fingers. As with alcohol, wasting a cigarette was not an
option. I couldn't understand why she'd make us drink but
wouldn't bother to feed us. Big C even had me smoke marijuana
on one occasion.

    I've often thought back to these times and wished Janice
had called a cab for herself and left me with my father after I was

born. If I only existed for her to torture, what was the point of having me around? I didn't like her, and she obviously didn't like me. She gave me the creeps. She was brutal and loud, she constantly used profanity, and she lacked intelligence in areas that were common sense to a two-year-old. I don't know what traumas she experienced during her youth that went unresolved and became catalysts behind her hysteria. I do know that the traumas I experienced while living with her went untreated yet have not caused me to torture any innocent people.

The extent of her drug use and drinking during the time we spent in this residence is still unknown to me. I can confirm that while I was force-fed alcohol and marijuana during that time, I have never used any drugs or drank alcohol since then. Not even a cigarette. The only good thing I learned from being around Janice was seeing an example of a person I never wanted to be like.

Big C never struck my sister or me. She beat her own kids, but never us. I think that in her mind, hitting us would have been the same thing as hitting Janice and their bond would never permit her to do such a thing. Her husband, on the other hand, would beat the hell out of all of us. He beat us more than Janice, probably because he was home more than she was. He'd make all five of us line up in size order and face the sofa. Then we would lean over with our elbows on the sofa, our knees on the floor and our rear ends sticking out. At this point he'd rain down on all of us with a leather belt. The belt fell on our backs, buttocks and legs. The worst part about being whipped like this was that you didn't know when to brace yourself for a strike. He never called out a warning during his beatings; you just felt it. If he felt one of us had committed an offense, he'd shout at that person from another room saying, "Have your panties down when I get there!" I once stood in a room for a long time crying with my underwear down waiting for my beating but he never showed up. The anticipation alone would wreck my nerves. On another occasion, I ended up alone with him in the apartment. My cousins were staying with a family member for a week, and Cheryl was out with Janice for a few days after being rushed to the hospital from an injury she got during innocent play with my cousins. I was starving and there was no food for me to steal. By this time, I'd learned how to climb on the top of the stove without burning myself to search for drops of spilled food. When Big C's husband caught me, he picked me up by my arm, held me in mid-air and tore into me with his belt. He was too strong for me to pull away from his grasp, so there was no escape. After what felt like an eternity, he dropped me on the concrete floor and left me there, sobbing. While he and Janice were responsible for the majority of my beatings, the worst violence I experienced during this period was at the hands of another child.

From what I could tell, she was a young teenager who, upon Big C's request, would come over to "babysit" us occasionally when the adults were gone. I cannot, for the life of me, remember what her face looked like, which played to her advantage later on. She basically came over to torture us. She would use a different method on Cheryl, Mitch and Ron while subjecting Yvonne and me to the same routine. She would pick me up by my hair and slam my head into the refrigerator repeatedly. My body would be whipping around like I was a ragdoll as she focused on gripping my head and getting enough momentum to effectively meet her target. Then she would make me pull down my underwear, lie on the concrete kitchen floor, and stomp me in my vagina balancing on one foot. She'd always be wearing those cowboy boots with the wooden heels, which hurt like hell. The first time she did this to me, I actually didn't cry. I looked up at her in a state of disbelief. How was this possible? What had I done to her? Why was she like this? She just kept stomping away like some mad woman. After this, she'd sit on my chest and put a butcher knife to my throat, marking it as if she were cutting me. What I hated most was when she'd involve me in sexual perversions that I still have trouble talking about. She was the first person I hated.

We were all very afraid of her. We'd try hiding before she came in, hoping she'd assume we just weren't there. We'd go under the beds, hide in closets or slide into the kitchen cupboards. I remember little Ron lying patiently on a closet floor while we covered him up with dozens of old shoes that were inside. She always managed to find us. On one occasion, she was beating Mitch up in the living room and he began to fight her back. She responded by hitting him even harder, but he still kept trying to swing at her. He was crying so hard as she continued to rain down heavy blows, but he wouldn't give up. Something snapped in me. My cousin didn't deserve this. He knew he couldn't win but he was trying to defend himself anyway. At that moment, getting punched and kicked by her didn't seem as bad as watching her beat him. I'd had enough. I jumped up and started swinging at her too. I'd never fought anyone before, but I was furious. She was fighting both of us, but we didn't care. Soon after, the other three kids jumped on her. We got some good licks in, but eventually she was able to get all of us off of her. I was thrown into a wall before falling to the floor. When the grown-ups came home, she told on us and we got our courage beaten out of us. Sadly, things went back to normal and we never challenged her again.

During one of the "throat-cutting" rituals that I was being subjected to, Big C walked in and saw what was happening. She pretended she hadn't seen a thing and instead told the girl that there was someone in the hall who wanted to speak to her. When she left, Big C locked the door behind her. She never "babysat" us again. Big C was crying as we began telling her all the things that had been done to each of us. I actually tried to tell Janice what was happening on the first night that I'd been stomped, but she didn't care. We had all tried to tell Big C what was happening as well, but she'd never believed us.

It turns out that during that time in our "babysitter's" life, her biological father was raping her on a regular basis. Later on I heard she ended up giving birth to two children conceived during these rapes. Today I can't say that I hold any hate in my heart for that girl. I don't know what became of her, but I hope her journey in life led her to a place of healing from the nightmare she'd been living for years before she became a part of my own nightmare. I don't condone her actions in any way, but I must take into account that she was a child who was being viciously brutalized before I pass judgment on her.

Having her banned from the apartment was a big weight off my shoulders. Janice still made me drink alcohol, but by this time I only saw her occasionally. Big C never hit me and while her husband did, he, like the other two grown-ups, began coming home less frequently. The constant struggle was trying to feed our hungry bellies. Drinking water from the faucet took care of the thirst, but starving for food was a daily thing. I really should have died from some of the stunts I pulled to get something to eat. GOD has been so merciful to me. I ate the sulfur tips of matches. One night I swallowed all the baby aspirin from a medicine bottle, fell asleep and woke up the following night. I remember being "it" while we were playing tag one day, and I spotted a half-eaten chicken bone under the table. I chased all the kids out of the kitchen, and once they were gone I went under the table, grabbed the chicken leg, brushed the roaches off of it and finished what was left. Those roaches probably never forgave me, but I was starving. They're lucky I didn't eat them as well.

The worst thing I remember eating was at the house of some man whom Janice introduced as my new father. He had a huge Doberman pinscher that was much taller than I was. Before Janice and this man went into a bedroom to have sex, she instructed me to pick up a cast-iron pot and hit the dog with it if he tried to bite me. Then she put some of the food they had been eating in the dog's bowl and left it on the floor in front of me. The dog's food was still in the bowl along with mine. I remember being alarmed at the distinct flavor of dog food, which I'd never had until then, and wondering why this man didn't have any plates. The least Janice could have done was wash the dog's saliva and half-eaten food out of the bowl before serving mine in it. I just sat there on the floor eating my meal while she sexed my "new father." The dog never bothered me. We both fell asleep on the floor that night. It beat spending the evening with Janice.

With all that I'd suffered through in that place, Janice never took me to a doctor. She didn't take me to get checked out after Big C verified that I'd been stomped in my private area. I received no medical attention after suffering larger third-degree burns on my arm when I was shoved into the hot oven door. I was crying as I watched my skin fry on the oven door leaving me with a bleeding wound. It's a wonder that it didn't get infected seeing how I never got so much as a band-aid for it. I still have the scar today. Years later when I was applying for college, I had to get vaccinations that were supposed to be administered during my early years with Janice. The burning sensation I felt every time I went to pee wasn't pleasant, but I got used to it without crying after a long time. My chest hurt from my lingering cough, which sounded like a walrus barking. The only treatment I got for anything was some white, pasty liquid that Big C used to put in Yvonne's hair to treat the lice. Complaining about my ailments to Janice wouldn't do any good, so I didn't waste my breath. No check-ups, no vaccinations, no nothing. I was pretty much on my own.

Once in a blue moon, my dad, my grandmother (Janice's mother) or my aunt would visit us. When someone was coming over, the adults put us to work cleaning the apartment. We washed the walls and floors, and cleaned the kitchen. We washed our faces, put on clothes (a shirt), and ran a comb through our hair. Dad showed up on two occasions with presents for our birthdays. When Grandma or my aunt came over, they always gave us each a dollar. After they hugged and kissed us goodbye, Big C and Janice would take our dollars and ask us what we wanted from the store.

Each of us gave them an elaborate list of treats but when they showed up hours or days later, all we got were lollipops. Where did the rest of the money go? Your guess is as good as mine.

It was rare that Janice took Cheryl and me to visit Dad or Grandma. I would have preferred that we were picked up, because I hated going places with Janice. She'd make us squat between parked cars to urinate if we said we had to use the bathroom. One time, she had us on the train heading somewhere and she kept shoving me around as we were riding between the subway cars. She was drunk as usual, and I couldn't help but wonder how she could have missed how dangerous this was. I felt like I was going to fall on the tracks any second. Another time, she was randomly stopped by police, handcuffed, and taken into an office building that had a holding area. She cursed every police officer in there to hell and kept telling me to push her glasses up on her nose because they kept slipping down. I never found out why they approached her that day but the image of a drunken woman, smelling of urine, staggering down the street with two little girls would have made me question her as well.

We basically stayed in that stale, cold apartment. We spent our days with our cousins, looking for food, playing tag, watching *Little House on the Prairie*, *The Jackson 5ive* cartoon and other television shows. We played in the rubble that littered the entire apartment, which consisted of old shoes, dirty clothes, broken toys and random objects. We didn't go to school. There were no trips to the zoo or amusement parks. That was our life.

- CHAPTER 3 -

Round One

Something had to give. I could just feel it. I was so tired of it all. The beatings, the drama, being sick, cold and hungry all the time. I even stopped sleeping in the old, single mattress that the five of us shared in one of the bedrooms. It never had any sheets, pillows or blankets and it reeked of urine. I opted for the sofa in the living room instead. One night I was awakened by Janice who had come in after being out for what seemed like weeks. She'd cooked herself an entire plate of bacon and was about to eat it and watch television on the couch. I don't know if it was because I looked so tired and defeated that she took pity on me, or if she was too intoxicated to remember to be cruel. She let me lay where I was instead of ordering me back into the room and she even shared her bacon. I was too exhausted to get up. I didn't try to talk or make any sudden moves. I quietly accepted a little bacon, ate it and fell back asleep beside her. She was gone by the time I woke up the next morning.

The day that the nightmare finally began to draw to a close came out of nowhere. My father showed up unannounced. He'd never done that before. Janice had no time to make us wash our faces or put shirts on us, so we were sporting our typical appearances. We looked like children from a third-world country that you see on those "Feed the Children" television programs. We were happy to see Dad, but he was furious. It didn't take long to realize that he was mad at Janice because of the condition we were in. A screaming match started between them, and Dad was holding his own. When they argued at home, Janice was really the one yelling and cursing while Dad responded in a voice a bit louder than his regular volume. On that night, Janice was out of her league. I didn't know Dad could scream like that. I'd never seen him so angry. He took Cheryl and me by the hand and started marching us out of the apartment. Janice responded by grabbing our free hands and tugging us back towards her, but Dad wouldn't let us go. A tug of war ensued with both of them shouting all sorts of damnation at each other while tearing us apart. We started screaming from the pain when Big C quickly stepped in and grabbed us both in a bear hug, pulling us away from them. She ordered them to stop, saying, "Y'all gon' kill 'em!" She told them to take their discussion in her bedroom. In the meantime, she took us to the living room and held us as we cried in her arms on the sofa. She promised that she wouldn't let them tear us apart. They were in the room for quite some time before Dad emerged to talk to us. He explained that he wasn't going to take us that night but he'd return very soon to bring us home for a visit. As he left, all I could think of was how much I hoped he wouldn't forget about us.

Dad did come get us within a week or so, and we went home with him for what was supposed to be a weekend visit. I don't remember much about the visit other than the fact that he fed us, and I was extremely happy to be in his presence without Janice around. When he was getting us ready to leave so that Janice could pick us up, Cheryl started crying and said she didn't want to go back. Dad calmed her down and took us both into his room to talk. I remember him asking, "What's been going on?" At this point, Cheryl and I began telling him the horrors we'd been living through at Big C's place. We described the gruesome details of our experiences quite candidly, as if we were talking about the weather. We weren't halfway through before my father started crying. I mean he was *really* sobbing. Honest to GOD, I had no idea he was being affected so deeply by what we were saying, but that's exactly what was happening. I didn't even know he was capable of crying. We tried to comfort him but after he wiped his tears he adamantly announced, "It's finished. Y'all don't have to worry about getting hurt no more. Y'all staying with Dad." I wasn't expecting this. At best I thought maybe he'd threaten Janice into straightening up her act and possibly get her to feed us. I must admit that while I loved what he was saying, I was a little skeptical about how he would go about accomplishing this. Janice was violent. She'd definitely try to physically hurt him if he tried to keep us there. I'd only witnessed him restrain her before, so I wondered if he would fight back this time. If he wanted to keep us, he'd have to because tears and asking nicely would never work on Janice.

We finished our conversation and stayed up a little longer before Dad tucked us into bed. Later that night, Janice showed up with my grandparents. I suspect that she brought them along just in case we told Dad what had been happening to us. If so, she knew she probably wouldn't be able to take us out of there on her own. When they arrived, Janice asked where we were and Dad brought them to our bedroom, where we were sound asleep. He pointed at us and said to her, "There they are. You touch 'em, I'll kill you."

Going back and forth to court was a little confusing to me. I understood that we were there to make living with my father a permanent arrangement, but a lot of things that were going on made no sense. Different people kept asking us to tell them all the terrible things that were done to us while in Janice's custody. Why couldn't we just tell one person and let them give our story to everyone else? The fact that Janice and her lawyers were always in the same waiting area as we were was just stupid. This wasn't a friendly gathering. We were on opposing sides in a legal battle. My Aunt Elease (Grandma's older sister) had filed a petition to get custody of my three cousins, so she was there sometimes as well. She and Dad would sit together chatting about the cases. When I had to tell the judge about how I was sexually molested, Cheryl wasn't allowed in the courtroom and the only people present were the judge, Dad and myself. We sat at a long desk in the courtroom, as I did my best to tell him all the humiliating details. I wondered if he was a real judge. He was wearing a shirt and tie, but he didn't have a robe or a gavel. Thinking about it now, he was probably trying to look less intimidating to me so that I'd be more comfortable talking to him. If that were the case, it was not working. There were also some caseworkers that asked how I felt about seeing Janice. I didn't want to ever see her again, but if seeing her was mandatory, I wanted my father to be present. They seemed to want me to say something endearing about her, but that just wasn't going to happen.

On one occasion, Cheryl overheard Janice's lawyer tell her she needed to stop drinking until after the case was over to prove that she was a good mother. Cheryl told on them immediately.

How could Janice consistently show up to court drunk and seriously think the judge was going to believe her? That, along with our testimony, should have been enough but the case took forever. We'd sit in there for hours at a time. Sometimes I slept on the court benches with newspaper pulled over me because it was always so cold in there. What I hated more than anything was when they conducted a supervised visit between Janice and us. We were in a little room with a caseworker that always seemed to be trying to get us to say something nice about Janice, when all of a sudden she walked in. Dad wasn't there, so I was so terrified. I literally became nauseous at the sight of her. I was extremely embarrassed by the way she greeted Cheryl and me. She kissed my ear, for what seemed like a damn minute, with her disgusting tongue, which reeked of alcohol. I didn't return her "greeting" with a hug or a kiss at all. I just sat there frozen, looking blankly at the social worker that seemed touched by the disgusting display of affection. It was clear that I wanted to be away from Janice. Why, after all we'd told these people, did they insist on bringing her around us? Wasn't it obvious that there was something very wrong with her? Was everyone going crazy?

In addition to my testimony, my father had to take me to a gynecologist to determine the severity of the sexual molestation I'd suffered. At five years old, I couldn't articulate everything that had been done to me, nor did I want to, so undergoing a medical examination was necessary. I should have known something was up because Cheryl wasn't with us on the day he took me to get checked out. I thought we were just enjoying a little outing together. Dad even bought me some snacks. We ended up at Lincoln Hospital, and Dad didn't tell me why we were there until he was leading me to a room where a female doctor was waiting for us. He told me to go in the room and take my pants off for the doctor to make sure I was okay. He promised that he'd be right outside the door waiting and that she wasn't going to hurt me. I was shocked. Why didn't he tell me so that I could prepare myself for the ordeal? Any woman who's been to a gynecologist can attest to how colorful the experience can be. Maybe Dad didn't want my nerves to be shot from anxiety, but I can't imagine feeling any worse than I did when the doctor began to examine me. She was a black woman in her late twenties or early thirties from what I could tell. She spoke softly and wasn't rough with me at all, but I felt pure humiliation. How long would it be mandatory that I reveal my shame to lawyers, judges, caseworkers, and now medical professionals? I didn't know this lady. Why were people stomping, messing with, and examining my stuff? Who was granting all of these people access to my private area? Later that year when school started, Janice showed up to the house unannounced wanting to take a look as well. I still had my coat and book bag on, yet there I was again, spread eagle on the couch, pants down, with

Janice doing her own inspection. I preferred the GYN. I didn't want Janice touching me at all. If I even thought about the possibility of her showing up, it made me nervous. Sometimes the thought would frighten me so much that I'd pull Dad aside and beg him to make sure I never saw her again. I'd be sobbing in the bathroom, begging him to honor my request. Unfortunately, Dad did not want to deny Janice from coming to see us even after he won full custody. Thankfully, we didn't get frequent visits from her. In fact, from the time we went to live with my father until I was a junior in college, I only saw Janice on six occasions, three of which were of her choosing. It was six times too many.

- CHAPTER 4 -

Dad

Living with my father was great. He fed us every day. We wore clean clothes, which he washed by hand. He even learned to braid so he could do our hair. He'd never been a full-time, single parent so there was quite a bit of adjusting he had to do, but he was making it happen. He played with us and took us to parks and the zoo, where we rode an elephant. We went on paddleboat rides and we'd pick flowers and catch butterflies to bring home, then we let them fly around in the apartment. During our first trip to the movies, we saw "Pinocchio." My first concert was when Dad took us to see Diana Ross in Central Park. It began to rain sometime during the first night of the concert, but Diana promised she would be back the next day to do another show. She was standing on the stage in a beautiful gown blowing kisses to the crowd, but I was afraid that she would get electrocuted from using the microphone in the rain.

One of the most amazing things about my father was that he was a born educator. It was hard not to learn something while being around him because he was always doing something that looked interesting. He taught me how to play chess in 15 minutes when I was four, a lesson that had a major impact on my life. He taught us how to read using homemade flash cards. By the time I entered kindergarten, I was reading on a second grade reading level and creating my own little magazines with articles and illustrations. I was already writing in cursive while my classmates were just beginning to learn their colors.

Dad also taught us how to sew by hand. We would take fabric and reuse pillow stuffing to make our own little pillows and dolls. One of the most important things he taught us was how to cook. I guess after he found out how we were being starved at Big C's, he wanted to make sure we didn't have to depend on anyone, not even him, to feed ourselves. In fact, one of the first rules he gave us was to make sure we ate whenever we were hungry. He didn't care if it was during the wee hours of the morning. He kept the fridge stocked with fruit and snacks. Under his supervision, we would use a little stepladder to stand on as we carefully tended to the food we were preparing on the stove. We'd make pasta, hot dogs, and we even baked biscuits. By the time we were five and

six years old, we could make a steak dinner without him ever
having to check in on us.

Dad was also quite an artist. He could draw, paint and
sculpt. His specialty was making jewelry, which he sold as a street
vendor. I would watch him for hours while he made bracelets,
rings and necklaces. Sometimes he'd let us record on his tape
recorder, which fascinated me. He put a little radio in our room,
which was great for me, as I had come to love music. The only
thing I missed about living at Big C's (besides my three cousins)
was some of the music she played. The first music I ever
remember hearing was a song that she played a lot. The voice was
very distinct and the melody would often get stuck in my head. It
took me more than a decade to identify it, because I couldn't
remember any of the words. It turns out that the song was "Shake
Your Body Down to the Ground" and the singer was Michael
Jackson. "Don't Stop 'Til You Get Enough" was also on heavy
rotation in Big C's home, though I wouldn't be able to identify it
until I started studying Michael years later.

Of all that my father taught me, the most important lesson I
got from him was to always put GOD first. I feel that a parent
hasn't really done their job if they haven't tried to inspire their
child with the knowledge that a higher power exists. Dad studied
Islam and raised us to be Muslim as well. While I no longer
subscribe to a religion, putting the CREATOR above all else is a

detail about my life that I will never relinquish. No person, situation or event—not even the transition of death—can break my connection to my MAKER. I don't get swallowed up with all the details that religions use to explain what GOD is or how HE/SHE created everything. I do, however, recognize that there is an immortal, divine source of intelligence and energy that is greater than us. We certainly aren't the geniuses behind the wonders of creation. Humans are too preoccupied with starting wars based on currency, hair texture and pigmentation to take credit for creating anything other than chaos.

Dad had his hands full, being a full-time single parent for the first time. The fact that we were two little girls really put him in foreign territory. Sometimes he would take us to his big sister's home to visit. My aunt had four children: Rhonda, William, Chandler and Robin, whom we all called Shugie. Shugie is the closest thing to a big sister that I ever had. When we visited my aunt's home, it was Shugie who took care of us. She was only nine years older than me, but at 14 years old she chose to take on the responsibility of caring for us every time we stayed over for a weekend. She cooked for us, dressed us, washed and braided our hair. She took us to the games at her high school where she was a cheerleader. She taught me how to swim within a few minutes just by telling me what to do. She took us roller-skating and to Rye Playland. On one occasion, we almost missed the last bus home because we kept drenching each other in a large water fountain at the park's entrance. I'm still amazed at how Shugie, a popular teenager, would have her two little cousins accompany her to parties and outings, around all of her friends. The way she loved us and took care of us put a lot of people who call themselves "parents" to shame. The thing that made her time with us so special was that she wasn't obligated to do it. She chose it. She chose us. It's not often to come across a teenager as unselfish as she was. Throughout the years we haven't always agreed, but she definitely cared about me. At one point in my life, she treated me better than any other person I knew. I'm thankful that GOD blessed us with her.

Dad registered us for school and I almost had a meltdown on my first day. My teacher was great, but when she went on her prep period, a couple of young teaching assistants showed up to cover her class. When my teacher left, those girls started trying to make the kids engage in sexual activities, and all I could think of was what had been done to me. I started crying as I lay on the cot that had been assigned to me during naptime, hoping they wouldn't try to get me involved. Dad told me many years later that he was quite tickled when I came home after my first day and announced that I was quitting school. I'd never told him what had upset me that day and when I finally did, he was shocked. Thankfully, the girls didn't come back to our class after that day.

There was another element to being in school that I had never factored in: fighting. While I was very experienced in getting my behind kicked by adults, the thought of hand-to-hand combat with one of my peers never crossed my mind. I figured that since I never planned to hit anyone, no one would have a reason to hit me. Boy was I wrong. My first fight took place on a school bus when a boy kept punching me in my back as I was waiting to exit. I could see my father standing with the other parents outside the bus window. He caught sight of what was happening and quickly started making his way through the crowd towards the window. By the time he reached up to bang on the glass and get the boy's attention, I'd had enough of being punched. I turned around, threw my assailant into a seat and beat him down. When I finally made it off of the bus, I was sobbing. Dad came up to me, chuckling as he hugged me saying, "Why are you crying, baby, you won?" It's pretty funny when I picture it now, but the meaning behind it still makes me as sad as it did all those years ago. I didn't want to fight. I thought no one would hit me again after Dad got custody of us. Dad explained to me that people would try to start trouble with me occasionally during my entire life. If it was verbal attack, his philosophy was, "Let 'em talk." He instructed me, however, that as soon as a person put their hands on me, my orders were to "go to war," as he put it. He warned me that he wouldn't be with me 24 hours a day for my whole life and that there would be times when I would have to defend myself. He reassured me that he wouldn't get angry with me for defending myself. He would say, "Save my baby's life," adding that some people started fights with intentions to kill their opponents. I took what he said very seriously, and decided that I'd follow his protocol if and when I met with a situation that was violent in nature. The only problem was, now I was afraid of yet another thing. It didn't matter that physically I was disproportionally stronger than most kids in my age group. The idea that someone might want to attack me, even if I hadn't done anything to provoke them, was no longer something I associated solely with my antagonists at Big C's home. Anyone had the potential to do this. Knowing all this changed me. I subliminally put up a guard to always be prepared to defend myself just in case. I never bullied people or started fights in school, but if one came my way, I would finish it.

I did pretty well in school, though I never felt like I fit in much with the girls even though they weren't particularly cruel to me. They all seemed to have a delicate quality about themselves, which I lacked. I tried not to let this bother me, as it didn't seem to be particularly offensive to anyone, but I did wonder why I was different.

Dad was pretty laid back during those days, so besides Cheryl treating me like crap, I didn't have much to complain about. After Dad won full custody of us, we all sort of fell into a routine and let our guard down. Unfortunately, we were blindsided by one of the most traumatizing experiences of my childhood. Cheryl was seven and I was six years old when we were kidnapped.

A couple of women (one by the name of Sharon Champ) from the BCW (Bureau of Child Welfare) showed up to our school and told Cheryl that Dad sent them to bring us home. We may have had an early dismissal that day, I'm not sure, but there were a lot of other kids waiting for parents who hadn't arrived yet. Cheryl came and got me as I was exiting the building with my class. She said that the ladies from the court were taking us home. I didn't know these women and I remember hesitating, asking her if Dad said it was okay to go with them, and she responded "yes" with a tone of annoyance as if I should have already known. I followed her to where the women were waiting and got in the car.

I don't remember everything that the ladies said to us in the car, but at some point Cheryl became very agitated with them. She was trying to tell them that they were driving the wrong way. They told her they were taking a different route to our building. Cheryl kept looking out of the rear and side windows in search of a landmark or anything that looked familiar. When they finally stopped the car in front of a strange building, Cheryl went berserk. Whichever lie those horrible women told her in reference to where we were going didn't match with where we were. They kept saying that we were meeting my father inside of this building, but Cheryl wouldn't cooperate. They were dragging her as she was crying, kicking and screaming in attempts to get away. She kept yelling to me, "Joye, it's a trap!" An alarm went off in my head, but I couldn't fathom that they would really have a reason to want to trap us. I tried to get Cheryl to calm down because I didn't want them to hurt her, as she was biting and clawing at them. I also wanted to believe what they were saying, that my father was meeting us in this building. A trap? No, that couldn't be. I told myself to believe what they were telling me because it sounded better than what ended up being the awful truth.

They got us inside of the building where we were placed in a large, dim, open office space that was basically vacant. We sat in there for hours and were told periodically that my father was on his way. Cheryl was upset, and as time passed, I began to worry as well. They finally called us into one of the smaller offices saying Dad was on the phone. Cheryl took the phone from the lady and spoke to him. The only thing I recall her saying wasn't something directed at Dad, but at the woman who kept trying to get Cheryl to wrap up her conversation. She shouted, "Shut up lady, I'm talking to my Dad!" Years later, my father still had to laugh at the way Cheryl put that woman in check, though at the time there was no humor in the situation. I spoke to him briefly after Cheryl finished and he assured me everything would be fine. After we spoke to

41

him, they took us out of the building and we were put into another car. A woman who we'd never seen drove us for over an hour to what I found out years later was Long Island. She took us to a residence where a married couple with three children lived. I found it a bit peculiar that the kids fit the description and ages of my cousins at Big C's house. The driver told us we would be staying there that night because it was too late to take us home, and then she took off.

Let's get something straight: if your job description includes lying to kids in order to get them into your car then taking them somewhere other than their home, without their loving parents' permission, you are a kidnapper. We were clean, fed, safe, doing well in school, and very happy when they found us. I hope that the individuals responsible for doing this to us have since learned that their criminal actions did not do anyone justice. I pray that they are not out kidnapping other people's children as well.

Amazingly, I still believed what we'd been told. Dad had reassured me that everything would be fine, so I felt no reason to panic. I expected to stay the night and was confident that we'd return home the following day. We got dressed and headed out the next morning with the other kids to school. I assumed we were dropping them off first before they were to take us home. I got a little nervous when we went into the school and the foster mother spoke with people in the office. The next thing I knew, Cheryl was being ushered into a line with a class that was passing by in the hall. I finally got the message. Everything that had been told to me was a lie. They *did* steal us. It was a trap. They must have lied to the foster parents as well, because the woman who drove us there didn't show up that morning as she said she would. Registering us into a new school? They had no intentions of bringing us back to my father. There were permanent changes being made on my life, and the worst part was they took the one person in the world who I was sure loved me. I lost it.

I lunged towards Cheryl first to take her out of the line she was in and get us both out of there. Cheryl's spirits had been broken by the end of the previous night and she had almost no fight left in her. She tried to calm me down while holding on to me, but they ripped us apart and she was dragged away. That's when I really went crazy. This was the only time in my life that I was violent towards any teachers. I was kicking and swinging at anyone who tried to grab me. I was crying and screaming for my father as teachers and an assistant principal came out into the hall to find out what the commotion was about. There were four of them holding each of my limbs, trying to force me into a classroom, and they were failing miserably. I held onto the doorframe with my hands and feet and ordered them to let go of me. I didn't want to settle in. I didn't want a new life with the foster family or the new school. I wanted to go home to my father.

More members of the staff showed up to assist the people holding me. I was finally wrestled into the class and pinned into a seat at a round table in the back of the classroom. It was around the Christmas holiday and the kids were working on their letters to Santa. Needless to say, I had drawn their attention with my dramatic entrance. Their teacher tried to keep them working on their letters but they kept looking towards the back of the room, most likely trying to figure out if the lunatic (me) was going to stay in the classroom the whole time. A member of the staff with a take-charge attitude was dispatched to monitor me while the other adults tried to help keep the students on task. She told me that I was upsetting the other children and ordered me to calm down and write Santa a letter. Dad never brainwashed us into believing in Santa, the Easter Bunny, the Tooth Fairy or any other mythological creatures. I looked at this poor woman like she was a complete idiot and then screamed to the on-looking children, "He ain't real!" They froze and looked at the adults with an expression that read, "So it's true!" Some of them began to cry, which put the adults into a frenzy to console them by retelling the lie of Santa and complimenting them on their nicely illustrated letters. My personal jailer couldn't have been more annoyed. She shouted at me for upsetting the other children, but I didn't give one damn. As far as I was concerned, if it was okay to kidnap me and rob me of the life I knew and loved, Santa could go straight to hell.

I wish I could go back and apologize for all the havoc I caused that day at that school. Unfortunately, I have no memory of any of the names of the teachers or even the school. I have an enormous amount of respect for educators, and I'm sure that none of those people had a clue as to what my story was. This is why I encourage teachers to be patient, respectful and consistent with any student, because you never know what hell they experienced by the time they get to school.

That was the only day during the six-week period we were there that I caused any problems. I didn't make any trouble in the foster family's home either. Cheryl and I actually got along with the couple's three children. I quietly followed the routines and tried to make it through each day, though I missed my father terribly. I'd become a bit numb to the depressing situation we were in, as I waited to see what other door of hell was going to open up on us.

There were two teenage girls who babysat us on a couple of occasions during our time there and although they didn't hit us, they were very mean. No surprise there. They spoke to us with a nasty tone and made it clear they wanted nothing to do with us. They were nothing like Shugie. I remember during one evening, one of the girls scared the hell out of me when she turned over an hourglass and told me that when the sand ran out, Cheryl—who was sleeping in the next room—would die.

I learned to steer clear of both of them after that, except on one day when I heard them discussing a music video they were watching. One of them kept talking about how sexy "Billie Jean" was, causing the other girl to remind her that the song was called "Billie Jean." The man in the video was Michael Jackson. This was the first time I'd ever heard his name. I'd never seen a music video before. I kept my distance as I peeked in the living room to get my first glimpses of the video. I was amazed by what I saw. Michael Jackson looked so slick with his leather jacket and those wing-tip shoes, not to mention he could dance. I was quite spellbound by his energy and I promised myself that I would find a way to see that video again as soon as I got the opportunity. That was the happiest I'd been since we'd been stolen.

Cheryl and I would ask the foster parents about when our father was coming to get us, and they told us it would take a while but that eventually he would. I had faith in what they said because everything else they told us seemed to be the truth. They really were good people, but when my father finally called and said he was coming to pick us up, we couldn't have been happier. The kids were a little sad that we were leaving, but they were happy for us at the same time because they knew how important our father was to us. When he showed up at the door, it was better than winning the jackpot. Boy was he a sight for sore eyes. He scooped us up, hugged us and the world was all right again. He brought us a couple of huge dolls that were almost as big as we were, but him being there was the real present. He graciously thanked the foster parents for their hospitality and even spoke to the children, but we were gone within 15 minutes. It felt so good to be home with Dad again. We spent that night eating and piecing together the details that led up to the kidnapping. According to Dad, when he got to our school on the day of the kidnapping, the school had no idea that we'd been taken. They were making announcements on the loudspeaker to locate us but we were well out of reach by then. By the end of the day, he'd found out that the BCW was responsible, but they wouldn't tell him where we were. They allowed him to speak to us on the phone, but they got us out of their office soon after in case he tried to come take us back. He told us that he had to focus on not panicking, which is what they wanted him to do. Cheryl told him that she figured out it was a trap early on because they lied to her about driving us home. She'd never given me any details about what had been said to her, so when they told me Dad was going to meet us there, I assumed it was true. He wasn't happy to hear how they'd dragged her into the building, but he was proud of Cheryl for sassing the woman about the phone call. I also had to explain to Cheryl why I was raising hell when they took us to school that first day. She thought I knew what was happening to us but that I just didn't care. Her theory never made sense to me. Why wouldn't I care that someone was stealing us from Dad? I've often thought back on the day we were taken and kicked myself for following her in the first place. Looking at the big picture, it would have been more traumatic if she'd been abducted alone, so it's probably better that I was there with her.

Dad also gave us a thorough breakdown of how he was able to get us back that night. He realized on the day that we were taken, that it was crucial for him to stay calm and formulate a plan quickly. He chose to pick up one of the most powerful weapons to fight the individuals responsible for the whole mess: a pen. Dad wrote the boss of the judge who had handled our custody case. Then he wrote that person's boss and so on. The kidnapping appeared in two newspapers, one of which was the Amsterdam News. He even wrote the White House and threatened to press charges on President Reagan if he allowed the criminal actions of the BCW and the judicial figures involved in the kidnapping to go unpunished. He showed us copies of the letters in which he described in detail the documented abuse we'd suffered and why he rightfully deserved custody of us. Then he showed up to the courthouse one day to check the status, and he spotted a Fed. (You know, those federal government officials who wear suits that cost more than your entire wardrobe.) As soon as Dad spotted this guy, he knew he was going to get us back. He didn't even bother with the judge. He walked straight over to the official who said, "Mr. Harper, we need you to stop writing letters." Dad responded with one question, "Are y'all going to give me my kids back?" The answer was yes and the guy even said they would bring us home to him, but my father didn't want to wait. He gave the address to Dad, who thanked him and headed to Long Island to pick us up.

That night, the three of us sat back laughing and talking like old Army buddies. We began to refer to ourselves as the Three Musketeers. I really miss that man. When he was around, he seemed to bring out the best in people. Cheryl didn't even focus on being mean to me in Dad's presence. She adored him. He wasn't just our father. He was our friend.

- CHAPTER 5 -

Lemonade

Life went back to normal after we came home from Long Island. We went to school and hung out with Dad who continued to educate us about the world and where he'd come from. He would take us up to Fordham Road where he sold his handmade children's bracelets on the street. Cheryl and I would wear them and model them a little in-between eating slices of pizza at what used to be the best pizza shop in NYC. Since my aunt's home was close, we'd often swing by to visit Shugie. Sometimes we'd stay the night while Dad went out and worked some more. He really loved Shugie and was especially grateful to her for showing such initiative with us.

I never got any trauma counseling for all that had been happening to me. I never really got a chance to express my feelings about everything. To be honest, I was so focused on moving forward that I didn't even have time to process how everything had been affecting me. I didn't want to focus on the horrors I'd been through. They were too frightening to think about. I wanted to move forward, get stronger and gain as much wisdom as possible so that those negative things could stay in the past where they belonged. I wanted to learn how to save people, especially children. I told Dad that I wanted to be a police officer, but after he gave me a lesson on police corruption and John Serpico, I switched my future occupation to becoming a doctor. I never likened my father to GOD, nor did I think of him as my idol (a concept I have never believed in), but I did want him to be proud of me. I once told him that my favorite color was red, but when he responded by saying that red was the color most commonly worn by prostitutes I changed my color to blue. It's pretty bizarre how parents can have such an influence on their children. There really is a fine line between offering guidance and indirectly controlling someone's way of thinking. A child's personality traits and behavioral patterns should be monitored, especially when they pose a danger to someone's safety. The problem is when an opinion gets classified as a law. While I'm sure my father meant no harm, I slowly allowed his influence to overrule textures of my personality in hopes that I'd become someone he'd approve of. There were a lot of things that came natural to me that didn't meet his approval.

These things I chose to hide or I just made alterations to fit his standards. Things like my favorite color were an easy fix. Other details, such as the fact that I wasn't heterosexual, would prove to be a bit more challenging for me to fake, as I got older. For the time being, things like that were left on the back burner. I planned on becoming a superhero, and I'd fall asleep fantasizing about saving the world every night. Dad would surely be proud of me if I could save people's lives.

Things went on pretty smoothly for about three years. I was one of the top students in my classes. There was no Janice. Cheryl and I were at peace about half the time we were in each other's presence and visiting Shugie was always a treat. There were a few fights with the neighborhood kids but nothing serious. The only major catastrophes I had were a pinched nerve in my neck and my bout with scarlet fever. Scarlet fever can damage the heart, but Dad never let on how serious it was, and I didn't investigate it until I was much older. It was the first time I remember getting a needle. I was crying and screaming bloody murder as four people held me face down on a hospital bed. Dad never left my side. In fact, I was holding on to his hair and we were both crying as the doctor gave me the injection with a large metal needle. I still appreciate how Dad was there for me that day.

When Cheryl started having trouble in school, Dad stepped up to the plate again. It turns out that she had been guessing the words in front of her. She couldn't actually read. She was held over in the third grade and when Dad went to a meeting to see what could be done, he was given the impression that Cheryl was a lost cause. Dad was not accepting that. Over the course of a few months, he tutored her one-on-one in reading comprehension. He called another meeting at the school to demand that she be placed back in her proper grade. I wish I'd been there to see him march into the office with Cheryl, hand her the principal's copy of *The New York Times* and have her read it in front of everyone. They had no choice but to promote her to the fourth grade where she belonged. It's amazing how she ended up being an author after having so much trouble with literacy in her early years.

The most challenging part of my life was trying to peacefully coexist with my sister. Dad instructed us to equally share TV time, snacks or anything else, but if Cheryl didn't get what she wanted, regardless of whether her way was fair, she'd start calling me names and being nasty. Sometimes she just said mean things randomly. I never reciprocated and sometimes I'd just let her have her way, simply because I didn't feel like being bothered with her yapping. As her vocabulary grew, her verbal assaults became more elaborate. She would say she hated me, call me a dog or a prostitute. She would even wish me dead or hope that I got diabetes. It got to the point where I couldn't take it anymore. She would start her rants and I'd ignore her until I felt like dying inside from what she was saying. I would punch her in her legs very hard when I felt like this. She wouldn't hit me back, but she'd collapse into a ball of sobs while continuing to damn me. This wasn't my reaction every time she spewed her hateful words, but I was still wrong for behaving in a violent manner on those occasions. It's completely unjust to physically assault someone who insults you. What she was doing showed poor character, but what I was doing was criminal. I never made her bleed or broke any bones. I never punched her in her face. The truth is I didn't want to do any permanent damage to her. I wanted her to stop hating me so much. It broke my heart to live with someone who would play with me one minute then wish that I be shot the next. The only name she called me that applied was when she'd call me a homosexual, which I was still in hiding about, partially because I didn't quite understand my own sexuality fully. I tried telling Dad, but she never received any serious punishment. After a while it must have sounded like two kids arguing to him because he would complain that our "fussing" was stressing him out. He would warn Cheryl to stop talking to me like that or one day she'd need me and I wouldn't be there for her. On the occasions that I acted out my frustration in violence, he'd tell me to keep my hands off of his child. Years later, I decided that I wouldn't lay a finger on her no matter what she said, in hopes that her verbal abuse would stop. It only got worse.

Dad wasn't seriously dating anyone around this time and if
he was, he never brought her around us. He didn't want us seeing a
string of different women coming in and out of the house.
Unbeknownst to us, Dad really wanted a woman in his life to help
him raise us. He was sitting in his room one evening, asking GOD
to send him such a woman, when there was a knock at the door.
Cheryl and I weren't used to getting visitors so we were extremely
curious to see who it was. We peeked our heads out from behind
our door to watch as a woman walked down the hall into Dad's
room. She was short with perfect dark skin, and she had on a suit
and glasses. Cheryl and I chatted quietly to each other about our
first impressions of her. She looked a little mean, though we'd only
seen her profile. We hadn't gotten a really good look at her, and
we anxiously waited until Dad finally called us in to introduce us
to Jodie. We practically galloped in to meet her. Once we were
face to face, we could see how beautiful she was. Her smile was
amazing. She was actually very friendly as she greeted us and
shook our hands. I didn't say it, but my mind was focused on one
thing. I wanted this lady to be my mother. I'd never felt that way
about any woman. As far as I was concerned, Dad was my mother,
but I'd never known what it was like to have a real mommy, you
know? From the moment I met Jodie, I hoped that she would
become our mom.

She stayed over that night…with my father. Dad and Jodie
started seeing each other regularly and they fell in love. She spent
so much time at our place that eventually she just moved in, which
was not what she initially intended. There was only one problem
with Jodie. The fact that she was 22 years younger than Dad could
be worked out. The problem was that Dad used to be a pimp and,
according to him, Jodie's mother had been one of his "girls." This
was a considerable glitch. Dad had already told us about his
gallivanting when he was a young man. Growing up fast and being
in the street didn't help. He wasn't stupid but he admitted to quite a
few stupid choices that he'd made in his life. These choices
contributed to why I'm still not sure how many siblings I have.
Dad was into girls and partying when he was growing up. He was
6'4" with green eyes and light skin, which played to his advantage
with the ladies. By the time Jodie came into our lives, he'd already
had six living children that I knew of. Tanya was the oldest, born
on Dad's birthday. Her mom Yvette was the love of his life, but
he'd gotten another girl pregnant at the same time that Yvette was
carrying Tanya. He ended up marrying the second girl, and from
their union my sister Towana and my brother Randy Jr. were born.
Years later they separated and Dad met a woman named Patricia
Threet who became pregnant with his child, but they parted ways
and Dad never knew what became of her or the baby. Cheryl was
next and exactly 11 months later I was born. Janice actually gave

birth to my brother, Thomas, when she was 15 years old, but he died very early on. I'm not sure if he even made it to a year.

Having painted this picture, you can imagine the type of guy my father was before he had us. He was actually in the process of turning his life around for the better when he met Janice. He stayed informed about activism in America and around the world, and educated himself about events and politics. Through a spiritual rebirth, study and applying himself creatively, he wasn't the same man that Jodie's mother knew when Jodie was a little girl.

I didn't find out until many years later, but on the first night that Jodie had stayed over with my father, she'd had a huge argument with her mother and was looking to get back at her. Though I know the details behind their dispute, I'm not at liberty to talk about them. I can say that Jodie's actions, inappropriate as they were, did not come without excessive provocation. At the same time, I believe my father should have used more discretion in the situation. The natural connection that Dad and Jodie had was something that they never saw coming, and soon she became a part of our family. We all loved her. To be honest, Jodie was the closest I ever got to experience what it might be like to have a mom. She played with us, read to us at night, cooked for us, braided our hair, made us clothes and even took us to school. The four of us would play in the snow, have water fights and go on picnics in the park. Jodie was very intelligent. She was constantly reading, and studying French with her language cassettes. Dad once told me that when they were together, he read more books than he ever had in his life. This was ironic being that he'd belonged to an organization called "The African American Book Club" during the '60s.

It was also Jodie who taught me how to lift weights properly. She had me curling 10-pound dumbbells by the time I was eight years old. She even attended our parent-teacher night conferences, and she took great care of us when we were sick. She was a parent, she did the best that she could, and she really loved us.

Things were pretty good for about a year, but it was only a matter of time before Jodie's expulsion from her family for being involved with Dad started to take a toll on her. She was stuck in a lose-lose situation. Her first option was to stay with her new family, who'd treated her with total appreciation, acceptance and love. The other option was to leave us and try to make amends with her old family, where there were already serious relationship issues that stemmed back to her childhood. Cheryl and I had no idea that this battle was going on inside her. It put a strain on her relationship with my father and resulted in her deciding she had to leave us before we became too attached. This was a huge blindside for Cheryl and me. I was actually sitting in our room, trying to think up the right words to ask Jodie if I could call her Mommy from then on. When I'd finally worked up the courage to go talk to her, she came into our room and told us she was leaving. She was crying and telling us that she loved us, but that it was best for all of us if she left. Her things were already packed and her mother was waiting, but we didn't care. We hugged her and held on, begging her not to leave us, but it was too late. She was sobbing as she left, and I was completely devastated. I had never cried that hard in my life, not even from the beatings. It may sound strange how I reacted to her leaving, seeing how I could care less about my biological mother being in my life. The best way I can explain it is to say that Janice never had my heart: Jodie did. I'd always wanted to know what it would be like to have a mommy, and Jodie ended up being my only chance. I guess I wasn't supposed to have one in this lifetime.

Jodie reconciled with my father and moved back in briefly, but she left again. This happened a couple of times, the last of which she was pregnant with my little brother Malik. The plan was for her to save up her paychecks to go towards a new apartment for us, while Dad covered the rent, food and bills. She got a place in New Jersey for herself and Malik instead. By this point, I'd stopped getting my hopes up that things would work out with her being a part of our family. She'd changed so much. On one occasion, she actually brought home a load of groceries for Thanksgiving and took them all with her when she headed back to

New Jersey to see her family. Cheryl and I came home from school and all the food was gone. Talk about invasion of the body snatchers. The Jodie we knew that first year would have never done something like that to us. I wasn't crying for her anymore.

She would bring Malik with her when she visited from time to time. She gave birth to my youngest brother, Kenyatta, a little over a year after she had Malik, but we never became the family that we'd once been.

- CHAPTER 6 -

Patterson Projects

The thing that was most troubling about Jodie leaving us was the change in my father. He became quick to temper and would yell at us excessively. I couldn't put my finger on why this was happening, but I knew that something was very wrong. Dad began to complain about how much stress we were giving him. He would question our loyalty to him, citing that he'd been our "bridge over troubled water" by rescuing us from Janice. It started sounding like we were a burden to him and that he didn't have to do what he'd done for us. Sometimes he would count down the years he had left to be committed to raising us. I didn't get it. Cheryl and I disagreed a lot and we argued every day, but the level of anger this would bring out of him wasn't normal. I was one of the top students in my school; I didn't curse, I wasn't fresh, I wasn't doing drugs or bullying people. By the time I was eight,

Dad didn't even take us to school anymore; we walked. The only time he had to go to school in reference to me was to get my report card, which was always excellent. He didn't even attend my award ceremonies or plays. Why had arguing with my sister, who regularly stated that I was a dog who she wanted to die, become a felony? His reactions made me not want to state my case when he was intervening during an argument. It was no use. He never really punished her for her verbal attacks; he just told her to stop doing it. I began to feel isolated.

Things went from bad to worse when we moved to Patterson Projects in the South Bronx. It was December of 1988 and I was 10 years old at the time. Cheryl was in the middle of her first year in junior high school in our old district. The plan was to have her transfer to I.S. 183—a school across the street from our new residence—the following school year, while I'd enter as a freshman. Until then, we would have to take a city bus to school. Our first night at Patterson, we ate Chinese food and cupcakes on the floor because we didn't have any furniture. The apartment was smaller than our old one and although we were on the first floor again, the windows were higher up so people couldn't walk by and look in.

The neighborhood was infested with gangs and crack dealers, so there were frequent conflicts. Unfortunately, a lot of conflicts resulted in violence, particularly gun violence. There was actually a shootout every night for the first year we lived there. We would have to "hit the deck" at the sound of gunfire. This meant stopping what we were doing and laying on the floor until the shootout was over. We got so accustomed to doing this that it became second nature. We could slide off of the couch or pillow-chair to lie on the floor without taking our eyes away from the television.

We met one of our neighbors, a woman named Katherine Jackson, soon after we moved into Patterson Projects. I've often reflected on the irony of MJ's mother and her having the same name. She lived in the apartment directly above ours and was a critical part of our building's tenant patrol association. She got Dad and me involved in it as well. Tenant patrol entailed tenants volunteering to take shifts in pairs, and having non-residents sign in at the lobby before going upstairs into our building. This discouraged the constant presence of drug dealers and junkies from hanging around the halls in our building. Ms. Jackson also saw to it that the housing management office was notified immediately if our elevator broke down, so that it could be prepared by the end of the day. She needed it more than any of us because she was confined to a wheelchair.

Ms. Jackson was an amazing person who knew how to live life. She went to Broadway plays and events, and she made it a point to be in church on Sunday. She ordered rose bushes and other flower plants for the three small gardens in front of our building and taught me how to care for them. My father trusted her enough to let us go to Central Park with her. Cheryl and I spent a lot of time with her, hanging out in front of the building or upstairs at her place. When my sister insulted me, Ms. Jackson would always look at her deeply and say, "Cheryl, that's not nice." She also told Cheryl that if she kept treating me that way, I might not be there for her in the future. Ms. Jackson was old enough to be my grandmother, but she'd become my best friend.

When I was finishing the fifth grade and preparing to graduate, a prep school program was presented to several students in my class, including myself. It offered to secure a full scholarship all the way through college. My father declined to enroll me in the program even though I wanted to go. He insisted that I would just go to the zone school across the street from where we then lived. In response, my educators offered to have me skipped a few grades and have me placed in the eighth grade the following year instead of the sixth. They argued that I would be bored with the curriculum, especially in the low-performing junior high school Dad wanted me to enroll into. I was reading entire textbooks and doing junior high school math by the time I was eight. They told him that I would be wasting my time in that school. Again my father refused. This really bothered me. I'd worked so hard, and having an opportunity to get ahead in my education was important to me. Unfortunately, this was not my decision. My sister was in her proper grade, though she wasn't producing exceptional results. When she'd gotten held over years before, my father busted his ass to get her back on track. Why would he hold me back from getting the best education possible? This just didn't seem fair.

On my last day of school, I said goodbye to my teachers and friends, some of which would be enjoying their rewards for five years of hard work in prep schools or placed a few grades ahead the following school year. I got home that day and couldn't find my most valuable baseball cards which one of my best friends, Ebenezer, had given me to start my own collection. Amongst them were Reggie Jackson, Willie Randolph and Rickey Henderson rookie cards. It turns out that Cheryl (who had no interest in baseball) took them to her junior high school to show off to people and had left them in her desk. I was crushed. Dad told her that she would have to buy me cards until she'd replaced the number of cards she'd lost, but she never did. I never stole from her and I didn't call her names. So why did she hate me so much and, more importantly, why wouldn't my father punish her? By the time we'd moved to the projects, her verbal assaults on me had taken a turn for the worst as she'd resorted to doing them publicly. Her vocabulary had matured quite a bit, thus her creativity in verbally bashing me had become monstrous. Dad let it be known from day one that us using profanity was not an option, regardless of whether or not he was present. Cheryl was smart enough not to resort to that (at least not within my earshot), but it didn't stop her from expertly humiliating me in front of people. I mean, she would seriously tear me up. I learned from years of being her target that effectively hurting a person's feelings could be accomplished easily without uttering a single curse word. She would wish out loud that I get murdered or say that she hoped I'd get raped or contract AIDS. She didn't let me forget how ugly I was and constantly called me a hooker. She even called me satan's wife, which she knew I hated, knowing my feelings about the devil. Character assassination is a common thing that can occur periodically in a person's life during disputes with adversaries. The thing that troubled me most about when Cheryl did it was that I actually loved her. I didn't take it nearly as personal when an outsider said bad things about or to me. But Cheryl mattered to me. I didn't earn her hatred, and yet she hated me nonetheless.

It was early August of our first summer in Patterson when I had a dream that Ms. Jackson died, and it was so upsetting that I told her about it the next day. She was supposed to be going on vacation in Canada the following day, and I told her I was afraid she was going to die in a plane crash. She laughed and told me she'd be traveling on a bus but that she wasn't afraid to travel on an airplane anyway. Her words were, "You just say your prayers, get up, and go…" She wasn't afraid to die and I'm guessing that this was why she wasn't afraid to *live*, wheelchair be damned. She made me feel a lot better by the end of the day. I wished her well that night and went home.

My father was heading out the following morning to get the public assistance money he received twice a month, but he came back in the apartment within five minutes and entered our room, looking very troubled. He said he had something to tell us and that we were not going to like it. I wasn't prepared for what he said next: Ms. Jackson was dead. She died of a stroke early that morning while sitting outside waiting for her bus to pick her up. I was devastated. I'd never lost someone who'd been so close to me. I was sobbing for hours at a time. Dad tried to console me when he was home because he could see that I was taking it very hard. A lot of people from the projects knew and loved her, and everyone in our building was distraught. She had been there for me as best as she could during the last year of her life. I would be starting junior high school in a few weeks but she wouldn't be there to see it, and I'd never get a chance to repay her for her kindness. I'm thankful that GOD sent her to this world if for no other reason than to remind people to not allow anything to stop them from living their lives.

Later on that week I was met with another catastrophe. I'd just gotten out of the shower and went into my room to get dressed for Ms. Jackson's wake. I took off my towel before sitting on my bed, and for a split second, I smelled something burning. Then I felt it under me. Cheryl had left a hot curling iron on my bed that she'd been using to curl her hair, and I sat right on it. I jumped up so high in the air that my head nearly caught the ceiling before I came down screaming. That kind of scream alerted my father immediately, who rushed in within seconds to kill whatever dinosaur had entered our room. Cheryl followed soon after, trying to explain that it had been an accident. I was sobbing from the excruciating pain as Dad went back and forth between trying to help me, inspecting my wound, and demanding to know why the fuck Cheryl left a hot curling iron on my bed in the first place. Cheryl said she'd only put it there to cool, which made no sense because we knew that Dad had a zero tolerance rule when it came to leaving sharp or hot objects in places where people sit or lay. He'd learned his lesson once when he almost lost his toes from leaving a butcher knife in the wrong place. He'd never been so furious with my sister, but there wasn't any time to get into a big discussion. Dad got me dressed and took me to Lincoln Hospital, which was only two blocks away. As strange as it may seem, what worried me most was that I wouldn't be done in time to get to Ms. Jackson's wake at all. The doctor gave me a huge needle and applied some sort of ointment on my wound. Finally he bandaged me up with gauze and some surgical tape, which was manufactured by satan and designed specifically to rip the skin off of me each time my bandages had to be changed. I could only sit on my left side because the third-degree burn extended from the back of my right thigh to the lower right buttock. I was told that it would heal eventually but that the scar it would leave was permanent. Thank goodness I had no plans of becoming a swimsuit model, though I would wear shorts to the pool for many years to hide my scar.

We got out of the hospital by the evening, and I quickly limped over to the funeral home for the last two hours of the wake. The place was full of people, most of whom I'd never seen in the eight months that I'd known Ms. Jackson. I literally saw her every day since we'd moved in. She'd touched so many people during the course of her life and I felt fortunate that I'd been a part of it. The next day, the three of us got dressed up and we went to the funeral. I was in a daze from grief. Dad was very patient and supportive with me. Cheryl and I didn't say much to each other. Dad still seemed annoyed with Cheryl because of what had happened to my leg. He didn't completely trust that it had been an accident, but given the situation and her insisting that she was innocent, he never punished her. To this day, she denies that she was acting maliciously. I still have my doubts.

During the weeks after the funeral, I had to stay in the house while Cheryl went out to play with her friends. My injury prevented me from being able to do anything rigorous without aggravating my torched leg. I'd lie on my stomach in the living room, on floor pillows, watching television all day. There were still nights when I cried myself to sleep missing Ms. Jackson. The rest of the summer went by without me really noticing much. I was used to the shootouts. Dad's mood swings had increased a little and Cheryl was as hateful as ever, but school would start soon. I figured that I'd bide my time and once I got into a rhythm, things would settle down.

- CHAPTER 7 -

Ghetto Children

I was late on my first day at Paul Robeson I.S. 183 because there was an issue with the records from my elementary school being transferred over. Dad had me wearing a skirt, which I hated because I always seemed to get into a fight or be put into a predicament that required athleticism when I had one on. I wasn't sure what was being said in the main office where Dad was getting my class assignment, but eventually one of the administrators led us to a full classroom and introduced us to my homeroom teacher, Mr. Hemans. He was tall, maybe an inch shorter than my father, and he wore glasses and had a mustache. They shook hands and spoke for maybe 30 seconds. I remember getting a strange vibe that they were very similar men in terms of their core objective, but their approaches were probably worlds apart. It was really a

71

sight: Mr. Hemans in his glasses, button-up shirt and khakis, and Dad in his camouflage jacket and hat, faded jeans and sneakers. Mr. Hemans' energy didn't come off as pompous, and my father didn't seem to react as if he were meeting someone who outranked him. They were brothers for that moment. It's funny how two very important men in my life never really got to know each other.

I spent that first day keeping to myself and trying to take in how things were done in this new environment. My keen ability to sense trouble allowed me to quickly pick out which kids to stay clear of, and there were many. I wasn't afraid of them, but I didn't want to get in a situation where I'd have to put one of them in the hospital. The school had its fair share of troublemakers, gangs, drug dealers and kids who carried weapons, including firearms. This place was nothing like my old school. It was actually one of the worst schools in the five boroughs. Dad turned down my entrance into a grade-A prep school for this? Great. I remember thinking how I wished he had let me be skipped a few grades so I'd only have to be in this place for a year. After the first week, I understood what my old teacher meant by saying I'd probably be bored academically in this new school. For the most part, the curriculum, especially the math, was review. Science class, which was taught by Mr. Hemans, was my favorite class, and I probably learned more there than in all the other classes combined. I was reading at a high school level by the time I was in the fifth grade, so language arts was a breeze. I kept my mouth shut, listened in class and did my assignments, not really expecting any special treatment. Why should I? I'd gotten my reward stolen from me after working so hard. Back to Plan A, I figured. Three years of this horrible school, then I'd be free to go to Bronx H.S. of Science, a specialized high school that I'd had my sights on since I was four.

Being that I had no expensive clothes or sneakers, it didn't take long before some kids started teasing me. I wasn't taught about girly things, hairstyles and things of that sort, so I was always a bit awkward. I made a few friends, amongst them were Zazy Lopez and Sol Santana. I wasn't popular amongst the kids who'd established any rank and Cheryl wouldn't be seen with me, so I was pretty much on my own. I did my best to ignore the idiots who had stupid things to say about my clothes and steered clear of the troublemakers who loved to start fights. I figured I could continue on like this and basically go unnoticed.

The first of four marking periods during the school year came to an end, and the dean announced that there would be a little awards ceremony. It was a bit of a shock to me that a school like this would reward students for good grades. The dean kept referring to some wonderful student who'd be getting a special at the end of the ceremony. Maybe I would find a new friend in this person. When they finally announced the award for the top student, my name was called, and I was shocked. I shyly got up to receive my award and the dean gave me two t-shirts along with my certificate. One was a Nelson Mandela t-shirt and the other was an African-American version of Bart Simpson. I'm almost certain that Mr. Hemans picked out the Mandela shirt. I gave high-fives to all of my teachers except the mean social studies teacher, Mr. Fenton, whom I faked out, which thrilled the rest of the kids. Years later, I grew to respect him as an educator even though his style didn't always resonate with his students. I went home that day feeling like I was someone who mattered in the world, even if it was just within the confines of that little school. Education was something that I valued and it felt good that someone thought it was worthy of recognition. At the same time, this little achievement had a down side, as it attracted attention of haters who now labeled me as "the one who thinks she's better than everybody." I continued to do my work and kept a low profile in attempts to minimize being subject to that kind of ridicule. I wore a poker face when we got our tests back and wouldn't let myself celebrate other small victories publicly. Mr. Fenton used to give us back our tests and make each of us announce our grades so he could enter them in his grade book. I hated this arrangement because while the majority of the class would call out mediocre or failing grades, my grade would be disproportionately high, which would earn me evil stares from some of the other students. Good behavior or grades could also earn a student small rewards such as "charge erasers," which were basically passes to get out of detention. I earned a lot of these, but I never used them for myself because I never had detention. Sometimes I just gave them away. There were a few of us, including Zazy Lopez who is now an attorney, that were considered the nerds who did well in school. We sort of gravitated toward each other and became friends. What separated me from the others and made me a target for constant teasing had little to do with my grades. I was ugly, my clothes were outdated and dingy, and my $20 sneakers didn't match up to the designer basketball sneakers everyone else was wearing. I carried all of my books every day, so the shelf life of my cheap book bags was about a month before they started falling apart. My book bags were always missing at least one strap and they had holes in them. I'd even developed severe callouses on my hands from carrying my strapless book bags in the frigid temperatures during the winter. I didn't know how to make my hair look pretty, and I didn't have any money. I'd also developed a chap line under my lower lip, which peeled and would bleed occasionally. I really was a train wreck back then. What I hated most was my coat. I think it was something my father had found, and it looked like it was in style back in 1970. Every time I walked by wearing it, people were laughing and making fun of me. Cheryl got a new coat because she'd grown out of her old one, but I was stuck wearing that hideous thing. I got so tired of dealing with people who bothered me about it that I would wait across the street from the school, away from everyone, until the morning bell rang. I'd wait until most of the kids went inside before rushing across the street and tearing it off immediately as I entered the building. The few friends I had never tormented me about my appearance, and the fact that they accepted me regardless of how hideous I was encouraged me. I never told them, but I'd secretly make note of the way they carried themselves like little ladies, as their mothers had taught them. I still felt awkward, but I made an attempt to take better care of the little I had. I didn't have fancy perfumes, shampoos and conditioners, but I did my best with deodorant, cheap lotions and hair grease. Lacking these things wasn't completely my fault, seeing how Dad never kept us stocked with toiletries. We were accustomed to using a single bar of soap for washing dishes, our bodies, hair and even our clothes if there was no detergent. With the $20 allowance I got every two weeks, I had to figure out how to budget for toiletries myself.

I actually got a little interruption from the teasing during that first year, when my big cousin Yvonne was enrolled at our school. She wasn't in my class, but she became popular very quickly and didn't have any fear in her heart. When it became known that she would gladly beat anybody's ass if they messed with her little cousins, I got a little bit of peace. It was short-lived because she transferred before the school year was even over.

It wasn't easy living in a place where the struggle for power between people who had almost nothing resulted in them victimizing each other. Through violence, sexuality or materialism, even the youth in our neighborhood were constantly trying to gain rank. Being part of a clique didn't necessarily save you from being a target. Sometimes fake friends within your group would look for opportunities to cut you down out of jealousy. I didn't think I had anything that would meet anyone's minimum standards, but this theory would prove to be erroneous from time to time. Once, Cheryl and I were hanging out with eight girls, who violently turned on us when they realized how long my hair was. By the end of the altercation, however, Cheryl and I weren't the ones crying with sore behinds. Something as trivial as long hair made me a target because it was a symbol of a female's beauty. Long hair was rare amongst African-American girls in our neighborhood because most of them used relaxers, which damages hair and the scalp. Many of them were trying to make themselves desirable to boys. A lot of these girls became sexually active during their preteens in attempts to get boys to want them. Teenage pregnancy was typical. Thankfully, my father had already made sure that I was well aware of every tactic a guy will use to try to pressure a girl into sex. He said that when I was old enough to find a mate, it wouldn't be someone I met on the street or at a club. I'd be better off finding a man in a library or at a university. He didn't want us to end up with the type of guy he himself used to be. Unfortunately, more than 90% of the girls in our neighborhood were without fathers. In fact, many of them had mothers who'd birthed them during their teens, which didn't help matters.

The crack dealers and gang members who'd turned our community into a war zone helped to promote a violent mentality amongst the youth as well. These traitors had no shame in resorting to gun violence to settle their petty disputes, even with children present. GOD help you if you accidently stepped on their prized sneakers or bumped into them. Such an offense could easily cause one of these dumbasses to pull out his gun and blow your brains out. One time, a gunman aimed his Uzi to shoot someone standing behind a few friends and me during a block party. He didn't care that he could have shot one of us, even though we'd done nothing to offend him. Until we'd moved to Patterson Projects, my only incident with drug dealers involved a gang of them "sicking" a pack of pit bulls on us as we exited a public pool when I was eight. Now I saw armed drug dealers every day. It's ironic how these same gun-toting idiots would put their tails between their legs and hide when police showed up. If police gunned down an innocent person, you didn't hear a peep out of these so-called "gangstas," but if you called one of them a bitch, he'd murder you.

I was still feeling the impact of losing Ms. Jackson, so when the tenants reassigned me to a new tenant patrol partner, I was a bit wary. For some stupid reason, I thought that I would bring bad luck to whoever took her place, but I accepted my new shift with Mrs. Eunice Reed. She was a little younger than Ms. Jackson and she also lived on the second floor. I'd seen her regularly and said hello in passing, but until then, we'd never really talked. She was very nice to me, and it didn't take long before she was inviting me to her home where she'd make me food and we'd talk for hours. Cheryl started to come along as well and "Aunt Eunice," as we would come to call her, soon became a very dear person in our lives. She and her husband, Uncle Willie, would give great advice and tell stories about their lives. Aunt Eunice really saved me on some days when I was feeling horrible. Sometimes I'd go run errands for her or go to the store to pick her up whatever she needed. When it got warmer, we'd go to the athletic field near Yankee Stadium and walk around the track for exercise. Dad had a lot of respect for her and appreciated that she opened her home to us. Something had changed in him and he wasn't the same cheerful guy from when we were little. He was stressed out more often, so it was good to be spending more time with Aunt Eunice to give Dad some space. It was also a good escape from being around Cheryl, being that I spent more time at Aunt Eunice's than Cheryl did. She didn't tolerate Cheryl's hateful words towards me in her house. With all the negative energy that was around me, I was thankful to have any positive people in my life. Aunt Eunice also had a daughter Sheila, who was a nurse, who visited her from time to time. She lived in Massachusetts with her husband and son, B.J. Aunt Eunice would often tell me how Sheila was set on becoming a nurse from the time she was a child, and that if I set my mind to my goals, I could make them happen as well. During the summer, Sheila met with Dad and arranged for Cheryl and I to come visit her in Massachusetts for two weeks. It was nice to get away from the projects for a while. Her community was clean, there where no shootouts, and the people didn't have an air of hostility. Sheila had a hectic schedule, but she found time to show me around the hospital she worked at. Her family was vegetarian, but she prepared wonderful meals that included soy meat substitute. I never thought I'd be content as a vegetarian, but after being introduced to this food, I promised myself that one day I'd adopt a no-meat diet. I was really impressed by Sheila, and I made it a point to stop by and catch up whenever she was visiting her mother. People like her represented what I hoped to become. She came from a poor neighborhood, but with focus and hard work, she was able to create a life she lived on her own terms. I knew that I wanted to live a life where I was able to help people and come home to a family that loved me. Part of me wanted to succeed in hopes of proving to my father that I was worth something. At the same time, another part of me felt compelled to put an end to the poisonous mentalities that led to humans mistreating each other.

- CHAPTER 8 -

Moses

Seventh grade started on a better note for 2 reasons: I already knew what to expect, and I'd grown out of that horrible coat. My grandfather (Janice's dad) would come by and visit every now and then, and this year he'd given us money for school clothes. Dad actually kept some of our money for himself, but what was left was just enough to buy a couple of outfits and some school supplies. Gran (Janice's mom) and Aunt Elease gave us money to buy sneakers. I bought a couple of outfits, a pair of British Knights and hoped that I'd be left alone for a while. My new homeroom teacher was an art teacher whom I'd often heard Cheryl talk about. Her name was Ms. Kupperman, but everyone called her Ms. Purple because it was her favorite color and much of what she had was purple. (Please note that her car was red—she was creative, not crazy.) I still had Mr. Hemans for science, so I wasn't completely disappointed, but I did miss him. His methods as an educator were top-notch. He was able to bring out the best in his students and he was fun. He also had a subtle way of promoting awareness of social justice and history by frequently wearing t-shirts with empowering images, African-American leaders and historical events on them. I learned something from him every day, which is why I wanted to be in his class. I must admit, however, that I really grew to love Ms. Kupperman. She was a bit of a character, but her personality added to her ability to engage the interest of her students. She taught me how to write in calligraphy, a lesson I still draw from. In fact, years later when I was in college, I'd get paid to write wedding invitations from what she'd taught me. My own penmanship looks like a doctor's handwriting, so it was nice to have this new skill. She was also one of the only educators I've ever come across who actually loved her students.

During the middle of that school year, I received a national award that was given to the top student in each school. I never found out who the best eighth-grade student was in our school during that time. All I know is that the faculty thought I deserved the award more. I continued to maintain the highest grades in the school and received certificates every marking period for my work. This didn't particularly make life any easier for me at home. For the most part, Cheryl was still randomly cruel, and though my father was glad that I was doing well, he didn't hesitate to frequently remind me that all my awards weren't worth anything if I didn't believe in GOD. I agreed with him, but I didn't understand why he continued to question my faith. He would regularly make accusations that my belief in GOD was just "talk" and that I was a cheap Jew. It was a perfect catch-22: if I failed, I'd be mad at myself and be classified as a loser; if I continued to do well, I'd be accused of valuing my personal achievements over my faith in GOD and be classified a loser. While the standards by which I took care of myself were slowly rising, my father's seemed to be declining. Even Cheryl allowed her side of our small room to be a total mess, while my side was as neat as I could make it. It was ironic how she'd spend hours in the mirror trying to make herself look perfect. She made sure she looked immaculate when she left the house but she could care less about her notebook, schoolwork or keeping her side of the room clean. She focused on trying to look beautiful. She would cut out hundreds of pictures of her favorite models and put them on her wall. She studied those models religiously and constantly talked about how fabulous they were. She talked about them so much that even I memorized some of their names. I didn't let her know, but I wondered what all the fuss was about over these women. She didn't look like any of them, at least not to me. She was tall and her skin was pale, which she considered one of the highest forms of beauty. People always said she and I looked exactly alike, commonly mistaking us for twins, yet Cheryl said I was hideous. According to her, she was the pretty light-skinned one and I was the ugly dark-skinned slave with burns all over my body. I wondered if Ford Model agency or Elite would see my face when she finally went to seek work at their companies. If so, I was sure she was a goner, because I never spotted any ugly dark-skinned slaves in the fashion magazines she'd collected. The dark-skinned women in the fashion spreads I saw were too pretty to be classified as such.

Cheryl was a bit of a mystery to me back then. I guess to some degree she still is. While she'd regularly let me know how much she hated me and wished I were dead, to her friends she would talk about how smart I was. She wouldn't even let me walk on the same side of the street as she was or she'd keep several yards of distance between us. Sometimes she'd put scissors, razor blades or needles in my bed sheets, hoping to draw blood. I'd gotten a 10-gallon fish tank from Mr. Hemans, who put me in charge of taking care of the wildlife he kept in the science classroom, during the holidays. Cheryl actually poisoned my fish once with Old Bay seasoning. She tried to deny it, but my father could smell the aroma of the seasoning and got very angry at her, stating that what she'd done was evil. I almost lost it on her once when she purposely tried to make me miss a citywide exam. Dad left early that morning and Cheryl was without her keys, having lost them. I was forced to wait for her before I could leave the house so that I could lock the door, not to mention that Dad told us to leave the house together. She purposely took her time getting ready and would have taken longer if I hadn't practically tossed her out the door. I stormed down the block to get to school as she shouted and threatened to tell on me. I didn't give a damn. She'd made me a half hour late to a test that she knew was important to me. She didn't care about school, but I had something to lose. I was in tears by the time I walked into the building. It wasn't common that I was late, but thankfully there were a few members of the staff who met me at the door and took me to a room on the main floor where I could take my test. I didn't get in trouble for that morning, and Dad got Cheryl a key. I ended up doing well on the exam, but I was very sore about what Cheryl had done for a long time.

One of the most disgusting habits she had was using any information I disclosed to her against me. We'd be having a civil moment where we could talk openly or exchange ideas. She'd listen to me talk and even give agreeable input. If a dispute came up days or even weeks later, she'd find a way to warp the details of our previous conversation in a way to mock me and make me sound like a fool. If my father insulted me within her earshot, or she found out about anything embarrassing happening to me, she'd laugh about it and bring it up at a later time. She also liked to lie about people who I thought were my friends, allegedly talking badly about me behind my back. She'd name Aunt Eunice, Dad and even Shugie.

She got very sick that winter from what she said was food poisoning at a local pizza shop. She lost a lot of weight and had to stay home for over a week. Dad waited on her hand and foot, and Aunt Eunice would come downstairs in the middle of the night with all kinds of teas and brews to make her well again. I playfully nicknamed her "The Witch Doctor" after that. I found out many years later that my sister wasn't suffering from food poisoning during that time. Cheryl had in fact taken 36 pills from six different bottles of medications in Dad's room and swallowed them in an attempt to kill herself.

I started to keep a journal as required by my English teacher, but I was hesitant to write my true feelings in it. I was afraid that my sister would steal it, read it and tell my father about it, so I basically wrote about my general routines. Every now and then I'd write about an out-of-the-ordinary occurrence, but my feelings stayed locked inside. I didn't have anyone to confide in who I felt could help me figure out what was happening with me, but I knew something was wrong. I loved my father, but our relationship had become turbulent. His abilities as a great mentor and educator coupled with his unpredictable mood swings, where he'd lash out with contradictions to some of his own teachings, left me at a loss as to how I should approach him. He loved me, but it felt as if it were by default because he had to. He didn't have the patience with me that he extended to Cheryl, and he kept accusing me of challenging his intelligence. One minute he was proud of me and the next he'd be calling me a cheap Jew because I didn't like sharing my toiletries with my sister who'd abuse them after squandering her own allowance. He was so talented, spiritually connected and captivating as a speaker. He had courage, and he was intelligent. Why did I bring out the worst in him? I'd been trying my best to adapt his opinions and general way of thinking as my own. I didn't act out when he'd refused my educational opportunities. I didn't rebel when he let my sister's hateful words against me go unpunished. I was trying to make my life work on his terms, but nothing satisfied him. I just wanted him to really love me and to think I was special.

I was sitting alone in the living room one day, looking out of the window, and reflecting on my life's purpose when a terrible revelation came over me: I didn't know who I was. I didn't know what my opinions were, and I realized that much of what I did and said was to prove my worthiness in the eyes of another person. This is what it means to be mentally enslaved. When you bend your mind and will so that they fall in alignment with the commands of another, you are a slave. I sat there crying while thinking about the few real things that were in my heart. I knew that I wanted to help people, and I knew that I didn't want to stay in the ghetto. I wanted a happy life.

I made a few life-changing decisions that day. First of all, I secretly decided that I would make a conscious effort to find out who I really was. This entailed me reflecting on situations, news stories and concepts that were brought up and identifying what I felt about them without being coached on what I should be thinking. I had to learn to use my common sense and think for myself. This also included details about how I saw myself and even my personal taste. This process would take many years, but it was worth it. Not knowing who you are leaves you open to being manipulated by those who love and hate you.

The second thing I vowed was to dedicate part of my life to helping people. It just didn't make sense for me to make a lot of money and build a great life for myself while letting everyone else suffer. If they knew that the option of liberation and happiness was within their reach, they wouldn't keep choosing misery. It was heartbreaking to watch people killing and hating each other and destroying their lives with drugs. The plight of victimized children would be a priority, not only because I knew their pain but also because they were the last people on Earth who deserved to be hurt. If I could find the right words to say and get people to listen, I could free them. The importance of not telegraphing a move was drilled into me and I knew it must be applied here. Much of what I would discover about myself would most definitely be misunderstood or rejected by my father and Cheryl. I had to keep my mouth shut about my ideas and wait until I was free to express them without facing daily opposition. It made no sense to make my life worse by giving my family fuel to ridicule me. There was no option to live elsewhere. I had no job, no money, and even if I did, I was intelligent enough to realize that I didn't know enough about the world to be on my own. This would have to change and be put into practice before the countdown to 18 drew to a close. I needed to be prepared when that day came. I promised myself that I'd find a job that year, even though it wasn't legal for me to work until I turned 14. I didn't care. I'd find a way. I already knew how to cook and do food shopping. Dad used to wake me up on the first Saturday of every month and send me to do the food shopping alone. Cheryl hated being seen with food stamps and she couldn't carry much anyway. I still don't know why Dad never came along to help. He used to repair shopping carts for an old lady in our building on a regular basis, but he never got me one. Usually I'd walk home carrying 15 or more bags of groceries from the supermarket. I always memorized the list instead of writing one. I was mature to some degree, but I knew it wasn't enough.

I didn't have much to work with, but at least I had a plan. In efforts to remind myself of this new sense of purpose and self-awareness, I decided to adopt a new name that would resonate with the energy I was seeking. It was on this day that I took on the name of Moses.

- CHAPTER 9 -

Thirteen

Thanks to my father, I'd been studying black history and African-American public figures since I was four. Most of the topics he covered weren't being thoroughly taught (if taught at all) in school. He would initiate history lessons on people like Malcolm X, John Serpico, General Mao, Gandhi and Harriet Tubman, from whom my name "Moses" was derived. I'd read at least seven books on Dr. King by the time I was 11, but Dad was able to fill me in with even more details about his life. I remember Dad being furious when the United States invaded Grenada for no good reason. He taught us that Europeans were responsible for most of the atrocities of human history and that this was just another example of them bossing innocent people around. Africa had been colonized and raped by Europeans. Europeans had stolen

America from its natives and had also colonized India. Hollywood constantly depicted prophets of the scriptures as being of Caucasian descent, yet the Bible flat out states that Moses, the original Hebrews and Jesus come from Africa. Dad really had a bone to pick with the *Crocodile Dundee* and *Tarzan* movies, citing that Africans and Australian natives were black people. While he would sing the praises of a few white Americans, such as John Brown or Marlon Brando, he openly stated that as a whole he didn't trust whites. They were troublemakers and their very nature was parasitic and brutal. I had my own feelings on the subject of race, but I wasn't at liberty to discuss them at the time.

Dad inspired me most when he talked about GOD. Years later, while studying the scriptures thoroughly on my own, I realized that Dad knew the Bible cold. Much of what I was reading, I'd already heard from him. He was often studying the Bible and the Quran, and he drew his teachings from both. He taught us that a real Christian, Jew or Muslim were basically the same in terms of the life they were supposed to be living. They were all supposed to be peaceful, loving and humble. He explained that there were notable differences between the three religions. Christians believe that Jesus is GOD. Jews deny that Jesus was the promised Messiah and maintain their belief in the GOD of Abraham. We as Muslims were taught to believe in the CREATOR of us all, ALLAH. He taught us that Muslims acknowledged Jesus as the Messiah but that he himself was not GOD.

All in all, I loved listening to my father give one of his talks. The combination of his expressions, voice fluctuations, gestures and energy gave him the ability to captivate a listener. I've studied orators and watched countless speeches, but no one I've ever seen had a style that resonated with more power than my father's. There are only a couple of people who've come close. It may sound biased coming from me, but I'm being honest. It's not difficult to detect similarities in the choreography used by a lot of preachers and motivational speakers during their delivery. Dad had a style that was all his own. My father had many flaws but his skill as a speaker remains unmatched, and I continue to draw from his techniques.

It was the end of the spring marking period and for the seventh consecutive time, I was ranked the top student. I looked forward to report card day although it had long ago become a meaningless inconvenience to my father, who didn't understand why he had to be the one to pick it up. My grades were wonderful. I had nothing to hide from my parent, so there was no need to take precautions that I might not bring my report card home to him. The principal and my teachers secretly waived this policy for me so that I wouldn't have to wait until my father felt like going across the street to pick it up. I remember that day well because we had a half-day and we'd be off for the next 11 days on spring break. Cheryl got home before me, but I wasn't ready for what was waiting when I opened the door. There, sitting on the couch, looking over Cheryl's report card was Janice.

My day was officially ruined. My father and I locked eyes for a moment, as a silent conversation took place between us. I asked, *Why is she here? You know I never want to see her again. Why didn't you warn me?* He answered, *I didn't know I was going to run into her, but don't worry. Poppa ain't gon' let her hurt you.* Cheryl was on edge as well, but even she knew to keep a lid on it until this woman left. When it came to Janice, the three of us had learned to never show division. That report card day happened to fall on Janice's 36th birthday. She was going over some of Cheryl's grades and making comparisons about how great she herself had been as a student in school, although she struggled in some of the same areas that Cheryl had trouble with. She kept saying to Cheryl, "You get that from me." I offered a little light conversation on the side with my father and exchanged nervous glances with Cheryl. I tried to excuse myself without pulling out my report card out, but Dad must not have heard my silent plea of, *Can we please wait 'til she leaves before we do this? I don't want her to start giving her point of view about my grades.* He wanted to see it, so I handed it to him, hoping he wouldn't make a big scene of it. He smiled and gave me a little high-five, noting that it looked like my typical marks, which were in the 90s. Janice asked him for it, and much to my displeasure he handed it over. She glanced at it for maybe five seconds then tossed it on the coffee table in front of her without saying a word. I didn't care whether or not she was happy for me. Her opinion meant nothing. I just wanted her gone. I went to my room and decided to stay there until she left. Unfortunately, Dad called for me to come say goodbye to Janice as she was leaving. Things got much worse when Janice went a step further, suggesting that Cheryl and I walk her to the train station and Dad agreed. What the hell was he thinking? I'd initiated countless private talks with him over the years in reference to me never wanting to be in her presence. Hadn't I literally begged him to keep her away from me? Apparently none of what I'd said mattered because before I knew it, Cheryl and I were walking outside with Janice. That was terrifying. We hadn't been left alone with her since I was four. I tried to walk on the other side of Cheryl, but Janice barged in between us. She suddenly used her body to accidentally bump into each of us and mumble, "Did you get your period yet?" We each answered no (though Cheryl secretly had), adding that Dad had long ago explained what it was. I didn't bother to mention that I'd already consulted my grandmother about why I hadn't gotten mine yet. Gran said that if it didn't come within the next year, she'd take me to a doctor to get checked out. Janice changed the subject to how good Cheryl was as a baby. She praised Cheryl and used this opportunity to take credit for how she'd cared for her as an infant. My sister was smart enough to maintain a level of passiveness while acknowledging what Janice was saying with an agreeable air so as not to aggravate her. Janice went on about how she was so happy to have Cheryl but that I was a pain in the ass that cried all the time. She said that she and my father never wanted me in the first place and she only had me so that Cheryl would have someone to play with. Cheryl was the one they really wanted. Finding out that Janice didn't want me was an understatement that made no difference to me, but including my father in this was just too much. I began to tear up. She smiled when she noticed this and taunted, "Look, she's about to cry," but Cheryl wasn't laughing. Neither of us responded, so she went on clucking about her own childhood memories and a slew of idiocies about her own greatness. For the first time in my life, I felt some of my fear of Janice lifting. The fear had no choice but to empty out a bit to make room for an indescribable rage that had just been born inside of me. This was the same kind of rage that pushes people over the edge right before they do something crazy. I didn't say anything, but my mind was in overdrive with what she'd said. This lady didn't know me. I wasn't a pain in the ass as a baby. I was an infant going through withdrawal having been an involuntary drug addict/alcoholic while in vitro. What made this insipid, stupid-ass fuck-up think that she had credentials that gave her the right to devalue my worth as a human being in this world? To her benefit, my allegiance to my father and how he'd raised me to be a respectful individual overpowered my urge to physically destroy her in that moment.

When we finally reached the train station, Cheryl and I politely said goodbye and even wished her a happy birthday. I can only remember a handful of times during my childhood that Cheryl came to my aid—this was one of them. As soon as Janice was out of sight, Cheryl started telling me not to listen to anything that Janice said. She kept insisting that Janice didn't know what she was talking about and that even if she didn't want me, she couldn't speak for Dad.

I was still upset when we got home, and Cheryl gave Dad a full report on how Janice had tormented me. She thought I was crying because the lies that Janice was spewing hurt my feelings. Dad came to his own conclusion that I was actually angry because I couldn't respond to her harsh words. He told me not to take any of Janice's harsh words to heart and that he only allowed us to go with her because we were now old enough to kick her ass if she physically got out of line. He even added that as we got older, we'd probably be closer to her than to him and that it would be okay to respectfully put her in check if she said something offensive. I was confused as to how my father was coming to all of these bogus conclusions for me instead of taking into account how I felt, not that he even cared to ask.

I'd dealt with name-calling and being tormented by my sister without him doing much to intervene. I was silent when he often dismissed my ideas. He and Cheryl were laughing at me when I told them that I would get a job that year, regardless of the age restrictions. I didn't ask him for extra money for clothes so that I wouldn't get picked on everyday. I didn't complain about his heavy restrictions that prevented us from going to parties or hanging out at a friend's house. In fact, the only request that I was consistently unwavering about since I started living with him was that he make sure Janice be kept as far away from me as possible. I was deathly afraid of her. My father knew this. He never signed me up for therapy to help me deal with my early childhood trauma, although unbeknownst to me, Cheryl had been seeing psychiatrists. I didn't ask for much from my father, yet on this day, my well-known feelings about Janice were disregarded. She was indeed the biggest object of my fear, which was saying a lot because I wasn't even afraid of the devil. I was angry with my father, but what I was feeling for Janice was a million times more deadly. I was beginning to hate her.

On the last day of school that year, Shugie came to meet up with us. She was finally home from college, having graduated that spring. When I caught sight of her walking up the block in our neighborhood, my heart celebrated. We peppered her with questions about her time in college and what she'd been up to. While at SUNY Binghamton, she'd studied and become fluent in Spanish. She even traveled to Spain for a while during her studies. She asked us how we were and even walked over to the school with us to meet some of our teachers. By the time we left that day, our principal had offered her a job as a Spanish teacher, which she accepted.

I was optimistic about starting the new school year simply because Shugie would be in the building. She'd be sure to hit it off big with the students. She was so wonderful, and I was really looking forward to her being around every day. At the same time, Cheryl was entering Art & Design High School. This meant I no longer had my self-imposed responsibility of looking after her when troublemakers tried to threaten her. Ever since elementary school, my friends knew that if there was ever a problem or an emergency with my sister, protocol was to get me immediately. On one occasion, a boy in her fourth-grade class kept spitting sunflower seed shells at her during the schoolyard lineup, while she responded by mouthing off about his entire lineage. A few of my friends caught sight of this and reported to me immediately before leading me to where they were. The boy was bigger than me, but that didn't stop me from decking him in front of his whole class. When he tried to lunge at me, my sister put him in a headlock. I guess she didn't want to fight him without me being there. The last time I got one of these reports was after her junior high school prom. Dad and I came to pick her up, and one of my classmates told me that Cheryl had tried to cut her wrist in the bathroom because a boy she liked wouldn't dance with her. I didn't even know Cheryl liked a boy. When I confronted her about it, she brushed it off and told us the girl was lying. She had a little cut on her arm, but she explained that it got caught on a broken bathroom door by accident. I let it go, knowing that the girl and my sister never got along. As she continued a more detailed explanation to put my dad's mind at ease, my classmate pulled me aside and warned me again to watch Cheryl. I thanked her for her concern and promised to look into it. Later, Dad asked me privately if I thought Cheryl was capable of something like that. I said no, stating that my friend was probably just mistaken, but my mind had enough doubt to keep a closer eye on her. I had plenty of thoughts and plans that I'd kept secret. It would be naïve to rule out the possibility that there was another side to my sister that didn't match the words and actions she expressed outwardly. I made a mental note to intensify the level of patience I showed her when she'd go off the deep end and lash out at me. This meant no more writing notes to my father asking him to make her stop talking to me the way she did. I would just wait until she ran out of gas and see if I could get her to trust me. It didn't matter how much she hated me. I had to help her. This world would most likely try to treat her like garbage when she grew up. I'd seen her suffer enough already. I was determined not to leave her side. It didn't seem right. Unfortunately, my approach seemed only to fuel the intensity of her rants. I'd sit in silence while she went off on me or I'd leave the room if I could no longer bear it. Sometimes I'd go into my room and punch my mattress until my knuckles bled. When she did it in front of people, they'd look at her like she was crazy or sometimes her friends tried to stop her. At this point, I would instruct the person to let her be until she was done. Once, she did this stunt at Shugie's house, and boy was that a mistake. Shugie never laid a hand on her, but she took her into another room and closed the door. My little cousins, Gina and Eugene, were there that night and we could faintly hear Shugie's voice, but we couldn't make out what she was saying. When they came back in, Cheryl was crying. It was years before I found out what was said. Shugie told her that one day she was going to need me and if she kept treating me that way, I would eventually want nothing to do with her. She also told her that as her sister, I was really all that she had in this world. She didn't have a mother, our other siblings weren't really in our lives and Dad wasn't going to be here forever. What would she do then? Cheryl still went ape on me when she was mad, but not in front of Shugie. After that day, I noticed that on rare occasions she would let me talk to her. It was usually me trying to inspire her about the great possibilities in life and having courage, as well as not allowing the way outsiders compared us make her feel worthless. I told her that she was priceless and she needed to believe in herself. During these talks, I often found myself listening to what I was saying as well, knowing that I too needed these reminders in order to stay encouraged.

- CHAPTER 10 -

Michael Jackson

My senior year in junior high school brought about a lot of changes. Cheryl and I were in separate schools, yet having Shugie in the building gave me a sense of security that I'd never felt at that school. Just knowing that there was someone close by who really loved me was more than enough, especially on my rough days. She would usually come home with me after school to hang out, or I'd see her during her lunch period. At the same time, I knew these kids were criminally wild at times and I felt I needed to protect her. She wasn't scared of anything, but I knew that this could attract the attention of the smart-mouth kids, some of whom would try to test her even if only to get a reaction out of me. What they didn't know was that in my mind, disrespecting my dear cousin was not an option. I'd been taunted mercilessly without reacting out of rage, but it soon became very clear that if someone so much as uttered a wrong word to her (or about her) in my presence, there was going to be a serious problem. It wasn't long before someone decided to test their luck.

Shugie was covering our class because our English teacher was out sick, and a boy sitting right next to me said something completely inappropriate to her. Without saying a word, I turned to him and punched him so hard that he flew out of his chair before landing on the floor. Everyone was shocked because I was always so quiet, but I didn't care. I didn't get into trouble for hitting the guy, but it wouldn't have mattered to me. I would have given my life to defend her honor. News of what I'd done spread like an epidemic throughout the school. That was the first and last time a student disrespected Shugie like that in my presence.

In addition to supermodels, Cheryl had started studying Michael Jackson. Dad seemed to regard Michael as a ridiculous character. He'd get into playful debates with Cheryl about Michael and started calling him "Pencil Nose." Listening to them go back and forth was pretty funny because my father seemed to be purposely trying to sound irrational and silly to get a rise out of Cheryl. I must admit that some of the things I'd overheard about Michael sounded rather disturbing. According to the press, he'd had 18 nose jobs, and bleached his skin because he didn't like being black. The elephant man's bones and hyperbaric chamber stories sounded pretty stupid to me, and even if they were true, that didn't make him strange. All I knew was that his music videos were the best I'd ever seen, his singing and dancing were amazing, and he often gave money away to charity. The plastic surgery stories bugged me quite a bit though. GOD made him perfect. He was beautiful. Why did he think he needed to fix anything? I wasn't sure what his story was, but his energy did not feel artificial. As an entertainer, Michael was all heart. I decided to find out more about this man.

As Cheryl started bringing home more magazine articles about him, I began to do my own research. We both collected articles and cut out pictures from magazines to put into scrapbooks. Cheryl borrowed books about him from her school library and eventually she would let me see them. She actually cut out all of the pictures from his autobiography before I got a chance to read it. After a long time, she gave me the mutilated book in exchange of doing some household chores for her. I went through the pile of papers from the slaughtered book, and one by one, I carefully taped them back together.

As I found out more about him, I was amazed at how much I could relate to his life as a poor black kid who'd been beaten and forced to grow up too fast. He'd lost his innocence so early, yet his faith in GOD was strong. His loneliness was on a level that I never wanted to experience. I'd known loneliness for my entire life, yet I knew that eventually I could escape it. All I had to do was wait until I was 18 so that I could move out and start a new life. Michael couldn't go anywhere on Earth without encountering people who either wanted something from him or would treat him like he was some character instead of like a person. This coupled with the fact that he'd been taught to live up to an image that pleased the public, instead of always doing what was in his heart, made it painfully obvious that he was a prisoner on this planet.

Around the time Michael Jackson released his album *Dangerous*, I finally got my first job mentoring kids after school at a church. Janet Avery, a businesswoman who brought her program to our school, trained a group of us in professionalism and work ethic. The goal was to get us prepared early for being part of the workforce. She was an awesome educator and a great inspiration for me because she wasn't limited to talking about a goal. She could produce results. When I got my first paycheck, I felt like I'd really accomplished something. Not only had I proven Cheryl and Dad wrong, but it gave me a sense of independence. I wasn't making much, but it was something. I got paid on the day before Thanksgiving and we were pretty low on food. As soon as I got my check, I went home and asked Dad to let me purchase all of the groceries needed to make the side dishes for dinner, leaving him to buy the turkey. He agreed without hesitation and I sensed that he was a bit relieved that he didn't have to ask me for the money. That evening, I cashed my check and went to the supermarket. It felt good to come home with bags of groceries that I bought with money that I'd earned. Dad warned me that the rent could be affected due to my new job, but it never happened because I wasn't making nearly enough money.

I got a second non-paying job at the school library as well. Ms. Weaver, the librarian, was very sweet. I don't know how many times she let me borrow Alex Haley's *Roots*. To date, I've read that book a dozen times. One Saturday, I actually read it twice. There weren't any books about Michael but if there had been, chances are I already had them. I used some of the money I was earning to purchase a small cassette player because I wanted to start my own collection of music. My best friend Zazy gave me three mix tapes she'd made herself, but the first music I ever bought was Michael Jackson's "Remember the Time" single. I played that damn thing to death. The "Black or White" video was released first and while I absolutely loved it, "Remember the Time" took my breath away. I appreciated the fact that Michael hired people of African descent to portray Africans. I loved the dancing. His singing was unreal and I was convinced that he was, hands down, the sexiest thing I'd ever seen. As I continued to get better insight on who he was as a person, it made me appreciate him more as an artist because it gave his work meaning. He gave away millions of dollars to charity, visited sick people, and his work included songs that campaigned for a healthy planet and peace for the human race. He wasn't just singing about it, he was doing it. After looking at the circumstances he'd dealt with all his life, it was a wonder that he hadn't lost his mind and pulled a damn gun on somebody. He was living proof that you could come from nothing and become a success without forgetting to care about someone other than yourself. In that respect, he was the kind of person I wanted to be. He was the kind of person I wanted to love.

When I'd saved up enough money to buy a small stereo with a CD player, my music collection began to grow considerably. Michael's albums were a priority, but other artists such as Queen Latifah (who is still my favorite rapper), Mary J. Blige, Jodeci, En Vogue and MC Lyte were all part of my collection. Most of the music I acquired by making mix tapes. I'd leave a blank cassette on standby to record in the tape deck and try to catch songs that were in heavy rotation on the radio. I'd listen to the 98.7 Kiss morning show, go to school and come home later from work in time to catch Wendy Williams do the "Top Eight at 8." I'd also record classics from artists like Gladys Knight, Carly Simon, Stevie Wonder, the Mamas & the Papas, and the Delfonics, just to name a few. Cheryl would be in the living room watching as much television as she wanted, while I'd be in our room delving into my own little musical world. There were times when I'd dance to Michael's music until I collapsed from exhaustion. Sometimes I'd just lie in bed and visualize my own stories to go with the songs. I'd picture myself rescuing people. I'd visualize families being reunited, scenarios of overcoming obstacles, battles— basically anything. It was almost like a slew of scenes from movies that didn't exist, coming to life in my head. There was something about great music that inspired hope and possibility in my heart. Sometimes I spent hours pressing rewind, just to hear one part of a song that moved me. I must have played the bridge of "I Don't Want to Do Wrong" by Gladys Knight at least a thousand times, just to hear that powerful string section. While I hadn't started writing hip-hop yet, I would practice rapping lyrics from my favorite songs. Queen Latifah's delivery was unmatched. I still can't finish the third verse of "Latifah's Had It Up 2 Here" without screaming. A Tribe Called Quest, Das EFX and MC Lyte were also amongst my favorites. They were all very different, but what they had in common was that they were lyricists who could cleverly tell stories with a vocabulary that wasn't limited to ghetto slang. Songs with crude, overly sexual lyrics that glorified stupidity and chaos weren't really my style. Once in a while, one of these songs would make the cut because of the instrumental, but I'd still be left wishing that the artist had done something better with it lyrically. A serious artist could express sensuality in a romantic song and do it with class. Great hip-hop artists could convey the harsh truths of urban life, their personal experiences and philosophies in a manner that was poetic and entertaining.

These people showed that it could be done. I'd think to myself how shameful it was that people died and struggled so that our generation would have a chance to hold the mic, yet there were people in the industry who ruined this opportunity. The industry was becoming infected with ungifted money seekers who called themselves recording artists. These were the sellouts that didn't think twice about exploiting socioeconomic traps set to contain the masses so that they could make a dollar. Michael Jackson was obviously not one of them.

I kept my love of music and dance to myself, so no one at school, except Shugie, had a clue that I had any talent. Since I was five years old, any time we spent the weekend with Shugie, I would always dance with her. Cheryl wasn't into it, but whenever Shugie put on music I'd be dancing up a storm with her. By the time I was 10, she was teaching me choreography that we'd practice in front of the mirrored wall in her living room. Janet Jackson's "Rhythm Nation" was one of our favorite songs to dance to.

It was during a school dance that my secret finally got out. The dance was held in our gymnasium, and there were several teachers in attendance to make sure the kids didn't expose any flesh when they started grinding, which was inevitable. I was standing on the side watching the other students when Shugie arrived. I followed her to the DJ's table where she asked him if he had Nice & Smooth's song, "Hip-Hop Junkies," which was on fire at the time. He did, and he agreed to play it on Shugie's signal. She thanked him and told him she'd be back in a few minutes. We left the dance floor and went to the girls' locker room, which was empty. I wasn't quite sure why we were there until she said, "Okay, so what are we gonna do?" We went over some dance moves we'd worked on and decided to do a variation of the "Bus Stop," which everyone now calls "The Electric Slide." Shugie changed the last half of the combination in a way that allowed us to get back into place to start the sequence over again. We did the whole thing a few times, locked in our spacing and headed back out to the dance. When we got there, Shugie caught the DJ's attention and gave him the signal. Once the song started, we made our way to the middle of the crowd. The students considered her the coolest teacher at our school, and it was no surprise that they were excited to see her join them on the dance floor. They formed a little circle around her to see what she would do. When I stepped into the circle to join her and we did her revised version of the combination, the kids lost it. We didn't pay much attention to them as we continued to dance, with Shugie rapping the lyrics as well. The crowd grew and cheered us on. When the song was over, she gave me a big hug, while students started flocking over to us to investigate what they'd just witnessed. My dancing shocked them. It never dawned on them that a "nerd" might know how to dance.

A few people asked me to show them what Shugie and I had just done. I did a few moves and they seemed really impressed. From that day on, my peers treated me with a different level of respect. During our lunch period, students would ask me to dance, and I even surprised them one day by speaking in an British accent. I didn't become best friends with any of my former antagonists, but it was good not to have to stress about constant teasing at school. The last part of my senior year was by far the best part of junior high school for me. Having my big cousin around really made life better for me.

I maintained the best GPA in the school for three years straight. I was working, and with Mr. Hemans' support, I'd started my own chess club. He also made it possible for the members of our medical club to get certified in standard first-aid and CPR. With all that was going on, the biggest surprise happened during an assembly that spring, when a radio station personality visited our school. He brought along a guy, whom we all assumed was a Jamaican comedian, to perform for us. The guy was wearing dark glasses, had long locks, and his jacket and hat had the colors of the Jamaican flag. He introduced himself and when the sound guy played a reggae song, he started doing a funny Jamaican dance, which amused the students. The song ended and when the laughter died down, he asked if we wanted to hear some American music. When we said yes, he turned his back to us and took off his glasses, jacket, wig and hat. When he turned back around to face us, he was dressed like Michael Jackson in the "Remember the Time" video. He floored the audience. I was speechless. The sound guy started the song and that man went to work. I'd never seen someone do an interpretation of Michael before. I'd been practicing in my room for quite some time, but I never thought that doing something like that on stage was an option. That guy was amazing. His whole performance was timed perfectly. From the Jamaican character to his MJ impersonation, he held the audience. They loved his dancing, and he even made them laugh. I promised myself that I would dance like that on stage one day. I wouldn't find out until years later, but the performer we'd seen that day was none other than CP Lacey, who's now considered one of the top celebrity impersonators in the world.

I selected Bronx Science as my first choice on my high school application. I would have to pass an entry exam to get into Science, and the grade director of our school, Mel Rabin, told me that I wouldn't get in because I'd probably fail the test. He said this with a big smile on his face and it was all I could do to keep from ripping the toupee off of his head. His comment suggested that he would personally gain something if I didn't succeed. If my demise would result in him receiving a cash prize of some sort, I decided to make sure he didn't get a penny. At the same time, Ms. Weaver and my gym teacher, Mr. Howard, sought out an amazing prep school program for me, which included a full college scholarship upon completion. I figured that this would be a great alternative just in case I didn't get into Bronx Science. My father wouldn't even go in to meet with them about it. In fact, he was angry with me for bringing it up and ordered me to stop telling him about opportunities of that nature because he was never going to give his consent. At one point, the school was sending letters and messages to him every day, asking him to reconsider but he never budged. In the end it didn't matter. Bronx Science offered me entrance into the school through their Discovery Summer Program.

During the last six weeks of school, I stayed busy with work, graduation rehearsals and writing my graduation speech. I'd been selected as class valedictorian. Shugie paid my senior dues, which covered my cap and gown, yearbook and prom fee. She also bought me a gold nameplate, which was the jewelry item selected for seniors instead of class rings. She took me shopping for my first suit as well as my prom dress. She even took me to get my ears pierced and bought an additional pair of gold hoops that I could wear after my ears healed.

As graduation day grew closer, I was particularly worried about my grandmother's health, which had gone into a rapid decline. Sometimes Cheryl and I would spend weekends at her house, and she'd make us dinners and special desserts that were unbelievable. She'd give us some money, when she had it, and she made sure that we memorized her phone number so that we could call her whenever we needed to. We didn't have a phone at home, but Gran instructed us on how to call her collect from a payphone. She was easy to talk to, very supportive and patient. She never raised her voice to us and she offered sound advice. I loved being around her and I often wondered how the hell Janice could be her child. Gran always said that she felt bad because she wasn't healthy enough to do more for us, especially since Janice wasn't in our lives.

I was calling her more frequently during the week before graduation. She wanted to go, but she needed a ride to the ceremony. My grandfather was going, but he hadn't offered her a ride. They'd been separated for over 20 years, but they were on good terms. Gran was too humble to ask him for a ride and she wouldn't let me ask for her, so I had no choice but to wait and see how it played out.

Stressing over everything resulted in me developing a nervous twitch in my fingers. Even in my sleep, my fingers wouldn't sit still. I also started to experience severe dizzy spells, especially during graduation rehearsals. Dad said that between school, work, clubs and everything else, I was spreading myself too thin. I needed to rest, but at the time it just didn't seem like an option.

On the morning of graduation day, Shugie came over early to do my hair and help me get ready. I was rather impressed with the way I looked, with my hair done and my new suit. Even Cheryl liked the way I looked, and her compliment would be the first of many that day.

After having almost perfect attendance for three years, it was ironic that I was running late on that day. It was my job to lead all of the graduates into the auditorium and when I arrived, they were all lined up waiting for me so that the ceremony could begin. As I walked up alongside them to get to the front of the line, they clapped, whistled and cheered me on, exclaiming at how pretty I looked. That felt nice. Shugie even took a few pictures of me with my best friend Zazy, who was salutatorian, before the ceremony began. I was eager to give my speech because it would be my first opportunity to address a large audience with a message that I wanted to give people. To my surprise, Shugie was appointed to give her own presentation to introduce me as class valedictorian. She praised my accomplishments and expressed how proud she was of me. I was once again overjoyed by how much my cousin really loved me.

Dad used to tell us that the idea of self-rule is the most powerful concept that could be taught to an oppressed people, and that's exactly what I spoke about during my speech. I encouraged my peers to have their own minds and to lead themselves. The fact that some people around us were choosing to fall into destructive patterns didn't mean we all had to follow them. To my surprise, I was met with spontaneous rounds of applause during my speech. I must admit that during those moments, more than anything, I was hoping that the graduates really heard what I was saying. I didn't care if they remembered me in the future. I just wanted them to heal and make better choices in life.

After the speeches were over, we received our diplomas and awards. My name was called so many times that the presenters had to ask the audience for shopping bags to help me carry all of my awards off of the stage. Shugie and Dad were taking dozens of pictures of me. The family members of other graduates were also coming over to take pictures with me and offer their congratulations.

One aspect of my life changed drastically on that day. Up until that day, guys never "checked me out." On my graduation day, it was as if a global ban on making a pass at me had expired. Grown men were actually stopping in their tracks to look at me and tell me I was beautiful. I was shocked, not only that they were doing this, but also that they were bold enough to do it in front of Shugie and Cheryl. In all honesty, I wasn't quite sure what they were looking at. I knew I was ugly, though this didn't bother me. All that had changed were my clothes and hair. I wasn't sure how to respond to these men. I figured that things would go back to normal after that day was over, but everyday since then, I've been subject to that kind of attention. Just another one of the pains of being a woman, I guess.

Later that night, I went to my prom and had a great time. Shugie was there and she took more pictures of me with my classmates as we danced. The only things missing from that day were my grandparents. My grandfather couldn't get into the graduation because he didn't have a ticket. He tried to argue that his granddaughter was the valedictorian, but whoever was at the door wouldn't budge. He never did offer Gran a ride and she'd become too sick to drive, so she didn't make it. She died exactly one week later.

- CHAPTER 11 -

Bronx Science

Losing my grandmother after finishing school on such a high note was a heavy blow. I was glad that she didn't have to suffer anymore, but she was one of the people I wanted to do special things for when I succeeded in life. I missed her dreadfully, and the realization that I would never be able to repay her for all she'd done for me made me feel lousy. Cheryl took it really hard as well. It didn't really hit her until Dad brought us to the funeral home because she was in a state of denial about the whole thing. She cried a lot on my grandfather's shoulder and at one point, he looked as if he would cry as well. I wondered if he felt guilty about not taking her to the graduation.

For an entire week, Gran's sisters and nephews were looking for Janice in the streets to let her know what had happened. It wasn't until the family had assembled at Gran's home after that burial that Dad and Janice's cousin, Raymond, finally located her. Her family lost track of her after Big C had died years before, but she would show up at a relative's home occasionally. It turns out that she was basically staying with different friends and hanging out in the streets with other addicts and alcoholics. When Dad and cousin Raymond called to say that they were bringing her back to the house, Aunt Edna (Gran's sister) joined the others in trying to come up with a strategy to handle her once she arrived. They were all on edge because Janice had a reputation for being a hothead and bringing drama with her wherever she went. I could care less. The last time I'd seen her was on her birthday when she tried to make me feel worthless. I went into my grandmother's room, lay on her bed and watched television by myself. I made up my mind that I wasn't moving from my spot until I was ready to, especially not for Janice.

It was obvious when she finally arrived. I could hear everyone moving about to greet her as she came in the door. I concentrated on the TV. Not 10 minutes had passed before I heard her voice, and she sounded agitated. She was telling her aunts that she didn't feel like talking and they were taking turns, following her from room to room, in attempts to console her. It was only a matter of time before she would come into Gran's room to evade them. When she finally did, neither one of us acknowledged the other as she took a seat in a chair near the window. We didn't say anything to each other, but it wasn't long before Aunt Lois entered the room and tried to talk to her again, causing her to get up to leave. I heard her saying that she was fine and that everyone trying to talk to her was what was aggravating her. She wanted to be left alone. I'm not sure how long the chase lasted, but eventually Dad and Cheryl ended up in Gran's room with me. Once things settled down a little, Janice came back into Gran's room and sat next to me. I'm not sure if it was in an attempt to be affectionate, but at one point she wrapped her fingers around my arm. She then gave my arm a little squeeze and shouted, "Damn!" Expecting a reaction to its muscularity, but wanting to force her to acknowledge it, I asked, "What's wrong with my arm?" to which she replied jokingly, "I'm hoping you won't hit me with it." At this, I returned with, "I hope so too." Cheryl was trying not to laugh while Dad pretended he hadn't heard and changed the subject. It didn't matter. I'd made my point. I was wearing a poker face as I thought to myself, *Yes, I'm stronger than you, and if you ever pull a stunt on me, I won't hesitate to do my best to fuck you up!*

We stayed over that night, with me on the loveseat, Dad on the sofa and Cheryl in Gran's room with Janice. The following day, Cheryl told me that Janice slept on her mother's floor and sobbed during most of the night. Cheryl didn't say a word to her, but she stroked her hair and looked after her as she wept. My sister has a way of feeling empathetic towards individuals, who are seemingly undeserving to others, during their time of need. It's one of the traits I believe she gets directly from GOD.

During that summer I worked for Janet Avery, and as a file clerk with Showtime Cable Network, in the accounts payable wing. It was nice to work in Midtown. I loved the energy of Manhattan, and it was cool to be the only kid working in the office handling invoices and checks. Once I got to deliver a $2 million check to one of our offices on another floor. The staff was great and I appreciated the way they respected me as a young adult. On one of my last days at Showtime, I finally got my period. I left work immediately and went straight home. My father could tell that something was up when I came in the door. I didn't say a word as I headed straight to the bathroom. Just before I closed the door, he asked, "What's wrong?" I answered by pointing to my stomach and shutting the bathroom door. He got the hint. I'm glad he did, because I had no intention of getting off of the toilet until the bleeding stopped or someone got me a sanitary napkin. I could hear him asking Cheryl to go to the store. While she was gone, Dad lingered outside the bathroom door and asked if I was all right. He didn't have first-hand experience, but he was intelligent enough to understand the significance of what was happening to me. Cheryl returned with the maxi pads and passed them to me when I cracked the door open. From then on, I set aside a part of my allowance for sanitary napkins, though my sister often used them without replacing them. If I had no money to buy more and my period came, I would use wash clothes or rip up a towel and stay home. A week after my first period, I started school at Bronx Science.

Science was very different from anything I'd ever experienced in school for several reasons. First of all, the student population looked like they represented the nations that make up the U.N. There were kids from China, Japan, India, South America, Africa, the West Indies, Europe, Korea, Saudi Arabia and other places on the map that I didn't even know existed. There were plenty of White-American students as well. Black Americans made up one of the smallest percentages of the student body. No surprise there. The students also came from different socioeconomic backgrounds, cultures and religions. In the mornings, all of the little cliques sectioned themselves off in the lunchroom to eat breakfast, finish homework, play Spades, nap or gamble until the first-period bell rang. There were kids with tattoos and strange piercings, who wore black makeup and called themselves "Goths." There were quite a few students who seemed to do nothing but study. There was also a group of kids who were obsessed with tossing around a Frisbee in the yard, just outside the lunchroom. They called it "Ultimate," which to this day I have no clue why they'd chosen such a powerful name for playing Frisbee. There was another group who played a game I'd never seen called

"Hacky Sack." This game entailed a small circle of individuals kicking the hell out of a beanbag without letting it touch the ground. Unless you were in training to learn how to do a kick like Michael Jackson, this game had no point. Most of the Black-American and Caribbean students sat on one side of the lunchroom, playing Spades and dominos. When I arrived in the morning, I sat at one of a couple of tables outside of their territory. I didn't think they'd accept me into their group, and they all seemed to know each other to some degree.

On my first day, I observed several kids amongst all the groups who were a little rowdy and used profanities. I wondered how long they would last in this school with that type of behavior. It was when I entered my first class that I figured it out. As soon as the teacher started talking, it was as if someone turned on a *"Shut Up and Pay Attention"* switch. Every student was quiet and paying attention to the instructor. People didn't go to class to goof off. When it was time to eat, they ate. When it was time to play, they played. When it was time to work, they *worked*. That was the biggest difference between Bronx Science and every other school I'd attended. The students were self-motivated and eager to learn, which is really what gives the school its reputation. The problem was that there were too many teachers amongst the staff who were experts in their subject but weak as educators, particularly in the math department. This coupled with the fact that I hadn't learned any new math since elementary school spelled disaster for me. Having stimulating educators was something I'd become accustomed to. For the first time in my life, I was an average student. This devastated me, as it seemed that now I had nothing. I was an awkward, poor, ugly, unpopular, average student. My home life was more or less as it had been, which did not help. I'd think about my situation and get angry with my father for not letting me go to a good middle school that would have prepared me better for Bronx Science. I didn't tell him this, of course. I just dealt with it. He wasn't required to pick up my report card anymore, and he never went to the parent teacher conferences in all my years at Science. When I brought home my first mediocre report card, he made light of it and just told me to study harder.

I think the first six months at Science would have gotten the best of me if it hadn't been for some of the new friends I had made. They were from different races, cultures and backgrounds, and not all of them were "A" students either. They were just nice kids who, like me, were trying to educate themselves and make some sense of their lives. Just being able to shoot the breeze and exchange ideas with people, without having to worry about being judged and criticized, was nourishing to my spirit. I'd spend the mornings talking with my friend Antoinette Noel, who was a wonderful singer and became the president of the a cappella club. My friend Laurie Mulhall was just naturally funny. I still have a birthday card she gave me that makes me laugh every time I even think of what she wrote inside. Having people with good energy around me gave me hope on days when I thought my despair might destroy me.

To be quite honest, after I stopped stressing about my grades, I was able to appreciate the overall peaceful energy at Science, which I was in desperate need of. I would wake up extra early to daydream for about 30 minutes, get dressed and leave the house before Cheryl and Dad were even out of bed. Usually I was one of the first 3 kids to arrive at school. I could feel my energy changing as I made my way to the building. I actually felt more relaxed at school than I did at home. I got a job in the school store and assisted in a chemistry lab during my free periods. I was elected by my homeroom as our class senator in the student government, a position I ended up holding for all four of my years in high school.

In the middle of the school year, the student government announced that there would be auditions for the annual talent show. I'd been practicing my dancing for quite a bit at this point and decided that this would be the perfect opportunity for me to perform publicly. I wasn't intimidated about performing in front of the school, as the students seemed to appreciate a wide range of arts and music in general. I did my audition in front of the talent show committee, which was made up of about a half dozen seniors. They seemed to like what they saw and settled on giving me a slot to perform in the show, which would be on May 26. I planned to dance to "Billie Jean." I began to sew silver sequins onto an old glove (a first of many) and started practicing more frequently. Dad knew about the show, but he was not going to attend. Cheryl wanted to go, but she wouldn't get out of her high school in time to see me perform. She did, however, agree to let me borrow her black fedora for my performance. It's funny how we seemed to automatically call a truce with almost anything regarding Michael Jackson. She was actually my biggest supporter during my early days on stage. Along with the hat, I'd be wearing black pants, a white button shirt, a leather black blazer that Shugie had given me, and penny loafers. Other than the hat, my outfit was inspired by the "Billie Jean" video.

I had butterflies on the day of the show, which was May 26, 1993. I was looking forward to it, but I guess nervous jitters just came with the territory. I'd performed in plays and as an orator in elementary school, but I'd never done a solo dance number on stage. After eighth period, I went to the auditorium and sat in my reserved seat with the other performers. I was psyched to see my stage name, Moses Harper, included in the program. By the time I got to Science, even my teachers called me Moses. The auditorium began to fill up and the show finally started. This was the first time that the performers got to see the other acts in the show, which included singers, steppers, musicians playing classical music, and even some East Indian dancers. My favorite act was this great rock band that did a cover of "Heart-Shaped Box," by Nirvana. I was enjoying the show overall, as was the audience who respectfully applauded each of the performers, as different as they were. There was no yelling or rowdy behavior during the performances, only a round of applause at the conclusion of each. I figured they would extend me the same courtesy, which put me at ease. A stagehand brought me backstage to wait on deck during the act that went on before me. When the act concluded, I positioned myself behind the curtains, put on the fedora and lowered my head. The announcer told the audience that a company sent Bronx Science a Michael Jackson micro toy to test out. To my surprise, his announcement earned a little applause. My heart was pounding, but there was no way out now. It was time. The curtains slowly opened and at the sight of me, the students responded immediately. I wasn't expecting a word from them until the song was over. The energy exchange between an audience and a performer can be powerful enough to have a lifelong effect on a person. It can heal you, curse you, or change the way you see the world. For me at that moment, all of my plans to become a surgeon went out of the window. I'd never felt anything like that. I chuckled to myself from under my hat, nervous jitters completely gone, as a friend approached me from the opposite end of the stage to "activate" me. The music

129

started and I began to move, causing the audience to explode. They were clapping, whistling and cheering as if they were at a concert. Dear GOD, what a beautiful feeling that was. One of the reasons Michael used so much energy on stage became clear to me. The only way he could possibly contend with the audience's energy would be to share a piece of his soul during a performance. Even if none of the viewers were drawing from the same place he was, their sheer numbers were enough to send a wave that could knock a weak performer off-kilter. Michael easily overpowered his audiences because the potency of his energy source, the CREATOR, is unmatched. I wasn't receiving waves nearly as strong as what he got on a regular night, but it was more than anything I'd experienced. By the time the song was over, the audience was on its feet giving me a standing ovation. I was exhausted, but the adrenaline pumping through me had me feeling like Wonder Woman. Backstage, people were hugging me and congratulating me on my performance. The crowd began chanting, "Michael!" so I went out for a brief curtain call. They gave me another round of applause when I was escorted to a reserved seat through a side entrance in the auditorium. I tried to sit quietly and watch the rest of the show, but people began making their way over to the section I was sitting in to congratulate me and ask me questions. They asked things like, *"Who's your manager?" "Where'd you get your glove?" "Are you related to Michael*

Jackson?" I answered them as best as I could, but what kept going through my mind was how much I wanted to get back on that stage. I wanted to dedicate part of my life to becoming an entertainer. I was naturally drawn to the arts for as long as I could remember. In addition to practicing on a regular basis, I'd been writing poetry, songs, and short stories as well as outlining plots for films. Scenes of possible film projects were commonly the themes of my early morning daydreaming. Maybe these things weren't coincidental. All of this was racing through my mind as students continued to ask me questions. An organizer for the B.O.S.S.—Black Organization for Student Strength—told me she wanted me to perform at their talent show on June 3. The show would be done Apollo-style, with an audience applause meter, which would determine the winner of a $150 prize. She assured me that I would win, but I needed no convincing. I wanted to be on stage. After the show ended, the dean came up to me and said that I stole the show. The principal also said he liked my dancing.

As I exited the school, I was met by a large crowd of students who had been waiting for me outside. I signed autographs, answered more questions and thanked them for the support. Things got a little out of hand when several of them tried to touch my glove and my jacket all at once. No one threw any punches, but the shoving and grabbing was a bit too much excitement for me.

I felt pretty good when I got home that day. Dad didn't come out to greet me, but he congratulated me from behind his closed bedroom door. Cheryl wasn't home yet, but when she arrived, I told her what happened and she was genuinely happy for me. She was so excited that she went back out to tell her friends about the show.

Back at school, I was greeted with dozens of compliments from students who'd seen my performance, my friends in particular. They knew I loved Michael Jackson, but they had no clue that I was a dancer. When the video of the show went on sale, I was the first to purchase it. We didn't have a VCR at home, but there were plenty of them in the classrooms at school. This was a real treat for me because I'd never seen what my MJ dancing looked like. There weren't any mirrors at home, so I would always use my shadow as a reference when practicing. Watching the video allowed me to finally see myself. There were a lot of small details and gestures that I'd been doing without realizing it, which really complemented my performance. I hadn't paid attention to these things consciously while studying Michael; they just came out naturally. My performance was far from perfect, but it was a start. I set my focus on the next show that would take place the following week.

On the day of the B.O.S.S. show, I actually forgot to bring my dance shoes to school. I went to an office immediately to call

Shugie. She spoke on my behalf to the administrators and they gave me permission to leave the school. She also said she would do her best to get to the show to support me. I rushed home, grabbed my shoes and returned to school as quickly as I could. When I arrived, I went to the auditorium immediately. All of the performers, none of whom I'd had the chance to meet yet, were there warming up. I didn't want to draw attention to myself, so I went towards the rear of the auditorium to stretch and practice a little. My efforts to keep a low profile failed when a few performers caught sight of me and stopped what they were doing to watch. A couple of them made their way over to me and introduced themselves. They seemed friendly enough, but I detected that the other acts were not as thrilled that I was there, judging by the worried looks they were giving me. This was a competition for a cash prize and they wanted to win.

Shugie showed up early, which put my mind at ease. She gave me a hug and wished me good luck before I went backstage. The performers couldn't watch the show and I was scheduled to go on towards the end, so I just hung around backstage and practiced to keep my legs warm. When the MC finally started to introduce me, I could hear whistles and shouts from the crowd. This show was public, so the audience was made up of a mixture of students as well as people who weren't from our school. I was positioned behind the curtains the same way I'd been a week earlier. When the curtains opened, the audience freaked. It wasn't long into my performance before they were on their feet, dancing, clapping and shouting. I got so excited that I went out into the audience to dance, but the people began to crowd me immediately. A guy working the event helped me get back onstage. Towards the end of my performance, I flung my hat into the wings as I'd seen Michael do, causing members of the audience to rush the stage in attempts to claim it. Thankfully, the host was able to retrieve the hat after my performance. As it was done at the Apollo Theater Amateur Night competitions, the acts began to file out one by one for the audience judging. The crowd was already chanting, "Michael!" before I stepped out on the stage. I won before the judging even began.

Shugie was super proud of me, and I felt like I'd done something really big. I was just a freshman, yet I'd beaten some very talented upper classmen, who were all more popular than I was. Maybe there was hope for me to fit in somewhere, even if it was on a stage.

I waited backstage until everyone left, as instructed by Officer Robinson, who was on security that day. She'd witnessed how wild the previous show was and judging by this crowd, she figured I'd get mobbed again. There were a few tears in the leather blazer I was wearing, from people grabbing at me during my brief interaction with the audience that night, but I wasn't hurt. Officer

Robinson pulled me to the side and told me that if I planned to do my act on a regular basis, I needed to think seriously about getting some bodyguards. It sounded a little silly to me at first for several reasons, one in particular. I wasn't Michael Jackson. I wasn't even famous, at least not outside of my school. After those two shows, I'd become one of the most recognized students at Bronx Science.

Tragedy struck again when my grandfather passed away that spring, exactly 11 months after Gran died. He had been sick for a long time, but he'd hidden it from us until the last minute. When I went to see him in the hospital, I couldn't believe the amount of pain he was in. He looked miserable. The only comfort I got out of visiting him was that I got a chance to say goodbye. I'd never gotten the chance with Gran or Ms. Jackson. Janice actually made it to my grandfather's funeral, but I kept my distance from her. Little did I know, I wouldn't see her again until I was 20 years old.

That year, I went to summer school to make up for a Regents math test I'd failed. By this point I'd accepted the fact that at this school, my best efforts earned grades that I considered average. I did my best and as long as I wasn't failing, I decided to stop stressing out over my grades. I had enough to stress about. In fact, the worst part of that summer had nothing to do with grades. It was August when a news story broke about charges being filed against Michael Jackson for sexual misconduct with a child.

Cheryl and I went berserk. I was pacing in front of the television for hours while coverage of the story dragged on. What worried me most was the likely possibility that he was surrounded by people who wouldn't have cared about him if he weren't Michael Jackson. It was obvious that the allegations were lies. Michael would never give a child a reason to hate him. Cheryl had followed media coverage of a few public appearances Michael made with his accuser, months before the charges came out. It wasn't out of the ordinary for Michael to be seen with kids, but Cheryl kept pointing him out and saying that there was something wrong with him. She kept saying he looked untrustworthy and didn't deserve Michael's attention. Boy did she hit the nail on the head. I thought she was just being jealous, but she argued that she never had a problem with Macaulay Culkin. To be honest, every person she pointed out as a perpetrator in Michael's camp ended up betraying him eventually. She has such an uncanny ability to point out sinister characters. Everyone will think she's being paranoid until eventually the guilty person is exposed for something terrible. Sometimes I think she would have made a good detective.

When school started again, it seemed like everyone wanted to get my assessment of the situation Michael was in. Sometimes a random idiot would see me from afar and call me a child molester, but nobody was stupid enough to start any real static with me. While I didn't appreciate their ignorance, what really bothered me was having to watch Michael get attacked on a global scale and not being able to do a damn thing about it. I was particularly disgusted when his older sister came out with her own claims that he was guilty. She later retracted her statements, but she's been on my shit list ever since she lied on him. My father seemed all but too eager to take her false claims as the truth. As far as he was concerned, Michael's skin, his plastic surgery and gentle demeanor spelled "faggot who wants to be white." I didn't like hearing the media vultures tear Michael apart, but living with someone who used every opportunity to bash him was worst. I knew better than to argue my opinion with my father, as he would only see it as a sign of disrespect and become angry. While he was entitled to his opinion, sometimes I wished he'd get the hint that I didn't want to hear it constantly. When the case was finally settled out of court, Dad said it proved that Michael was guilty. "Hush money" is what he called it. In my opinion, the settlement proved that Michael had been a victim of an extortion plot. What parent would accept money to drop charges against a criminal who hurt their child? To the contrary, a real parent would want the bastards responsible for attacking their child severely punished. No amount of money can undo psychological trauma suffered by a child who's been sexually abused. By definition, a person who accepts a fee in exchange of allowing someone to perform sexual acts with a third person, including a child, is the business of a pimp, not a parent. In pursuing a settlement, the accuser's father should have been brought up on charges for basically saying, "I won't have you put in jail for sexing my kid if you pay me." Disgusting.

During the annual talent shows, I performed "Remember the Time," wearing a gold satin turtleneck that I'd made. I insisted that the hosts announce that each of my performances were dedicated to the innocent Michael Jackson. It wasn't much, but it was my way of publicly stating my support of him.

- CHAPTER 12 -

Tangerine Summer

I refer to the summer of 1994 as the "Tangerine Summer" because the song "Tangerine," by Led Zeppelin, was stuck in my head almost every day I went to work. I was amongst several students who assisted in a field biology research program at my school. The job entailed gathering samples at the Botanical Gardens and Central Park, then bringing them back to school to be analyzed. I liked this job a lot because it was fun and it got me out of the house where tension between Dad and us had reached a new high. Anything could set him off. I forgot to wash the dishes once and received a 26-hour lecture on everything from cleanliness to the LORD ALMIGHTY. His mood swings were a way of life by this point, except on the days he got public assistance money and food stamps and would give each of us $20. He told me that when I started getting a paycheck, he was going to stop my allowance because it wasn't fair to Cheryl. I went with it—not that I had a

choice—but the only problem was that I hadn't gotten paid yet.
There was some mix-up in the system preventing the city from
sending out any of our paychecks. Needless to say, this delay was
irritating the hell out of my father. He kept giving me an angry
script to use when inquiring about where my money was. I told
him that our on-site supervisor wasn't the one in charge of the
money, but Dad didn't want to hear it. My father's erratic spurts of
anger made going to work worth it, pay or no pay. Cheryl wasn't
working but I figured out that if I didn't try to interact with her
when I got home, I could basically avoid her verbal abuse. Things
had gotten so bad with my father that even she was getting
annoyed with him. In attempts to get out of his way, we would
visit my older brother Randy, who we sometimes called "Pop." He
looked more like Dad than any of us, but they were very different
men. Randy had been working with troubled teens for years and
had a house full of his 10 adopted sons. He was a very loving
father, a basketball coach and highly respected in his community
for his outreach work. He lived in Yonkers, so we had to get
special permission from Dad before we could go visit him. Randy
would take us to the movies and treat us to anything we wanted to
eat, though he was an awesome cook. Sometimes we'd go to
basketball games he was coaching. His son actually taught me how
to dunk, though I stopped doing it because it always hurt my hand.
If Cheryl said something nasty to me, Randy would reprimand her

immediately, which was something I wasn't used to unless Shugie was around.

I loved my brother's energy. He was smart, and he had no fear in his heart. I wished that he'd been around when I was younger. At 16, I only had two more years left to survive before the countdown was over. Cheryl seemed to be at her wit's end with Dad's excessive irritability. One day she told me that she was going to ask Dad to let her spend the weekend at Randy's house and if he refused, she was going to run away to live with Randy for good. I asked her if she was sure she wanted to go that route but her mind was made up. I wondered if she was bluffing, yet I secretly hoped she would go if for no other reason than the fact that being around my brother had a positive affect on her. I wasn't there when Dad refused her request, but he honestly had no reason to turn her down. She'd done her chores, she wasn't on punishment, there was no school and Randy had invited her. I never found out why he said no, but my guess is that he was just doing it because he could. When I came home from work, Dad was gone and Cheryl was packing a few things she wanted to take with her to live with Randy. She left me the things she felt she no longer needed and told me that the room we'd shared was now all mine, which was fine by me. I knew that I could visit her any time I wanted to and that she'd be completely safe in my brother's home.

When my father returned, he asked for my sister's whereabouts. I did not lie to him. Cheryl said that it was okay for me to tell him the truth because she'd be long gone before he could do anything about it. My father's reaction was quite a shock. He stood in silence with tears in his eyes. He was crushed that she'd deliberately defied him. I told him that his unreasonable restrictions and anger had become too much for her. She wasn't off causing mischief. She was 17 years old and she just wanted to see her brother. There was no consoling him. He actually looked like his heart was broken, as if he'd lost her or something. He really loved Cheryl. Seeing him like that reminded me of how he looked once when Cheryl was late coming home from school. There'd been a water main break, which flooded the subway tunnels, and while no one was hurt, rerouting the commuters was causing delays and a lot of confusion. As we both stood watching the news coverage about the flooding, he said, "I wish it was you instead." I was puzzled at his remark, which seemed to blatantly indicate his disregard for my well-being. He caught himself and elaborated, saying that I would probably be able to maneuver better in a crisis situation and make it home safely. The matter at hand, however, was no accident. Cheryl meant business.

It took about a week before my brother brought her home. When they arrived, Randy went to Dad's room to speak to him privately. Dad never disrespected my brother in my presence, so I didn't expect any drama. My guess is that Randy was probably telling Dad to go easy on Cheryl, who was now in our room filling me in on the details about her stay at his house. Randy had been telling her stories about Dad, and one thing he told her was too unbelievable for her to wrap her head around. It was the reason why my father was always on edge. She kept hesitating when I asked her to tell me what it was because she wasn't sure whether or not it was true. She had a zero-tolerance policy for anyone who tried to badmouth her father, but she knew that Randy wasn't a liar. Finally she blurted it out, "Dad's on crack."

About three years prior to Cheryl running away, I remember going in my father's room to ask him a question. This was rare because we were never allowed to go in unless he said we could enter and his door was always shut. As I was turning to leave, having finished conversing with him, I spotted a clear glass tube smudged with smoke on the floor. It was a crack pipe. I never said anything about it to him, but now it made sense to me. A lot of things that had gone wrong suddenly made sense. Things like the decline in our relationship with him. The nights he'd wake us up to borrow money that he'd just given us as allowance that same day. The fact that he'd spend hours in his room, door shut, and forbidding us entry even if we needed to talk to him. He'd say he'd be right out or he'd just talk to us from behind his closed door.

When Randy finally left, it took Dad a while before he confronted Cheryl about disobeying him. I wasn't in on the conversation but it couldn't have been pleasant because Cheryl was in tears when it was over. She didn't let him know that she was aware of his addiction, but I remember thinking that it would only be a matter of time before it had to come out. Soon after that day, we found out that Shugie and Aunt Kim knew about Dad's drug problem, which is one of the reasons Shugie checked up on us so much. She advised us to call her and say "Code Nine" when Dad was spazzing out, to which she responded by inviting us to come spend the weekend with her. If we could get a hold of Shugie, this approach proved to be very effective because my father would never reject a request from us to spend time with her.

I began to brace myself for the day when our knowledge of my father's addiction would be out in the open. Knowing how self-righteous he could be, this would almost certainly cause all hell to break loose. He prided himself in being able to support his theories with scriptures. He never let me forget that all of my academic achievements were useless without having true faith, as he did. How was he going to explain this? To be honest, I didn't think any less of him for being a drug addict. I was afraid for his life. As far as I'd seen, crack was a poison that killed people. It didn't matter that the users experienced an extreme high when they smoked it. The trade-off obviously wasn't worth it. My father was well aware of all this. I couldn't imagine what in the world got him involved with something so stupid in the first place.

I decided that when he became aware that we knew his secret, I'd let him know that I still loved him but stress that I was completely against the drug itself. I didn't want him to feel like I looked down on him. Unfortunately, I wasn't mentally prepared for the series of events that brought everything out into the open.

It was August when the city finally mailed out the paychecks to the students who'd worked at my school that summer. Dad was the first to get to the mailbox, so I wasn't aware when mine arrived. He asked me to go to the store to get him cigarettes, which I'd stopped doing long ago because they caused cancer. He insisted that he had a surprise for me if I went, but I respectfully declined. I knew something was up because he was in a cheerful mood for no apparent reason. Finally, he presented me with a single piece of mail addressed to me, which he'd hidden. I'd already brought in the mail that day, so he must have sifted through it to find my check. He was waiting for me to get paid. The envelope was unopened but you could tell that there was a check inside. I opened it to see if I'd been paid the amount I'd estimated. It was a little over $500, which was about right. As I was inspecting it, Dad said he wanted to see it. I hesitated, causing him to give me a nasty look as he snatched the check from my hands. Seeing the figure seemed to set him at ease again.

I wanted to cash my paycheck immediately, but the check-cashing store wasn't open. My father didn't care. For hours, he and I marched all over the shopping district nearby, looking for a bank that would cash it. It was pouring rain that day and we had no umbrellas. The customer service reps kept explaining that they couldn't cash my check because I didn't have an account with any of them and even if I did, it would take a couple of days for the check to clear. It was four o'clock in the afternoon when Dad finally called off the search and we walked home. I would have to wait until Monday.

While I wasn't thrilled about having to wait, what bothered me most was seeing my father in such frenzy over money. He never showed that much interest in my schoolwork or me. He wouldn't even go across the street to pick up my report card. All he wanted from me that day was money so that he could get high. He didn't want to spend time with me. It broke my heart.

I called my Aunt Kim from a pay phone, told her the situation and asked her what I should do. She said not to give him any money when I cashed my check, because all he was going to do was smoke it. I thought about it and realized that Dad's welfare check, food stamps, and the rent check (which went directly to the rent office) had already come earlier that week. There was already food in the house, yet I intended to spend at least $100 of my earnings on more groceries in addition to giving my sister some money. We didn't have a phone and electricity in our housing project was included in the rent. There was no need to give Dad any money other than the $20 allowance he'd given me earlier that week.

I hated the fact that my father smoked cigarettes. I wouldn't even go to the store to get them for him. There was no way in hell I was going to help pay for his drug habit, especially with money I'd earned from busting my ass all summer.

I was at the check-cashing store across the street from our building as soon as it opened on Monday morning. To my surprise, Dad was right on my trail and met me as I exited the store. I handed him a $20 bill and he looked at it in horror as he exclaimed, "What's this?!" I told him that I was giving him back the allowance he'd given me earlier that week. He demanded $100 but I told him that the budget I'd come up with wouldn't allow me to do so. He glared at me, shocked and furious as I stood there with a poker face. I wasn't trying to come across as smug, nor did I want to show any sign of fear, though I must admit that he looked as if he were about to knock my head off. The contrast in our expressions must have looked pretty interesting to anyone who was watching. He kept screaming at me, saying that I needed to come up with another number, but I held my ground. In the end he snarled at me, calling me a cheap Jew, before storming off. I called my aunt and told her what had happened. She was astounded at the amount of money Dad demanded from me. When I went home and told Cheryl what happened, she was amazed that I'd stood up to Dad. He came back into the apartment minutes later and demanded again that I come up with a better figure to give him. I told him that the expenses in my budget wouldn't permit me to give him any extra cash. I needed to pay for school supplies, SAT fees, college application fees and clothes, none of which I expected him to help pay for. Cheryl was watching the whole scene in silence, but I could tell that she couldn't believe what she was seeing. I wasn't in the practice of defying my father, especially not to his face. I'd never even stated my anger or frustrations to him because I didn't want the backlash of being called ungrateful or weak.

The whole thing ended with him cursing me and bashing my character, then giving Cheryl the $20 to go buy sausages from the supermarket, so he could feed my "black ass." When he left, I told Cheryl to keep the grocery money before handing her an additional $20. I told her I would add the sausages to the list of items I planned to buy from the supermarket. This time, Cheryl went with me to the supermarket. We discussed the situation as we shopped and Cheryl listened to me more than she ever had in her life. I told her that I wasn't trying to be stingy. I wasn't trying to disobey my father. I didn't consider my refusal to support something that could kill him an act of malice. Even she couldn't deny the change that had taken place in him over the years, most of which we assumed was a result of his drug addiction. I reminded her that one of the first things he told us when he got custody of us was to get away from him if he ever started acting crazy like Janice or the people we'd been living with. I was just following his orders. My father wasn't perfect, but the Dad I'd known when I was a little girl and the person he was now were very different people. While she made it clear that she wasn't brave enough to do what I'd done, she'd also gained some respect for me for standing up for myself.

I ended up spending a little over $130 on groceries that day. I stayed in my room when he came home, hoping he'd take note of the overstocked fridge and cabinets, and praying he wouldn't summon me for another confrontation. He wasn't upset with Cheryl so she was free to interact with him, though according to her, he didn't say much.

Days passed without him talking to me. He told Cheryl that he felt like I betrayed him. I wanted to tell him my reason for not giving him the money he'd asked for, but Cheryl was afraid that he'd get mad at her for talking to me about it in the first place. I assured her that she'd be left blameless when I spoke to him about it. I carefully formulated my thoughts, organized my wording and did a bit of self-coaching before I finally got the nerve up to talk to him. He was in the living room, pliers in hand, working on a piece of jewelry, when I approached him. I told him that I loved him but that I knew he'd stepped into a "trap," a term he'd used in reference to a drug habit. I also stated that while I thought no less of him, much like his cigarette habit, I had no intentions of contributing to his use of this intoxicant that could ultimately kill him. It went against everything I believed in. He listened in silence, never taking his eyes from the piece of jewelry he was making. I'd stopped talking and was waiting for him to respond. Finally he looked at me, as if he were viewing a toilet full of diarrhea, and said that if he wanted to take a sniff of cocaine or any other intoxicant, it was none of my fucking business. He added that I needed to stay in a child's place and that GOD looks at the stride of a person, not their stumbles. This was one of his stumbles. It wasn't controlling him and he didn't have a problem. My job was to mind my business. He couldn't have said all this in an uglier tone than the one he used. I wanted to tell him that *he was my business*, but wisely decided against it. I finally got the hint. He didn't want to hear me.

Finding out that we were aware of his addiction actually backfired on us, particularly me. His great lectures on an interesting topic became far and too few in between. His attitude became nastier. He was paranoid that we were teaming up on him or conspiring against him. I'd think to myself, *What would we be conspiring to do?* He'd often wake us up, asking for money he'd given us earlier that day for allowance. I'd slept with my baseball bat in between my mattress and box spring for years just in case an intruder tried to attack us as we slept, but now it had a dual purpose. I wanted to be prepared to defend myself if drugs sent my father into a violent rage. This never happened. His accusations about me challenging him happened more frequently though, even if I voiced my opinion about something unrelated to either of us. He'd always be saying things like, "You think your shit smells sweet!" or, "Those white teachers got you brainwashed!" The most hurtful thing he'd say was that all I did was *talk* Islam. I didn't *live* it. Though I don't subscribe to a religion now, GOD has always been more important to me than anything or anyone. I felt like my father knew this and used it just to hurt me. Being the turncoat that she was, Cheryl would sometimes use the insults Dad hurled at me during his rants as fuel when we had an argument. When Dad said that I was in danger of becoming a homosexual, it was practically music to Cheryl's ears. He knew Cheryl would use what he was saying against me, but he didn't care. He'd sabotaged great opportunities for me in my education so that she wouldn't feel left behind, yet he threw caution to the wind when it came to humiliating me in front of her. She called me a homosexual so much that I wondered if she could hear my thoughts. I hadn't come to terms with my sexuality, having been taught that GOD would send all gays to hell. I continued to pretend that I hated gays as well and planned on staying a closeted bisexual for life.

I quickly fell into the rhythm of my hectic schedule during junior year at Bronx Science. I was in several clubs including the a cappella singing club, student government, and B.O.S.S. Between afterschool programs, work and school every day, I'd often get home as late as 8pm. It was common for me to walk in the door and the first thing I'd hear was Cheryl fussing at me to do the dishes. I'd think to myself, *I've been out all day. Would it have killed them to clean their own dishes?* The drama, the arguments and being yelled at were causing me an enormous amount of stress. Dad used to say that when you come home, you should be able to put down your sword, shield, and armor. If you couldn't do this, the place you lived in wasn't your home. In my case, I actually had to put more armor on when I got home. At school I felt safe and free to express myself. I had friends and people who supported my efforts. I was learning new concepts through being around the people at school, which allowed me to revise a lot of primitive ways of thinking that I'd been taught. Subscribing to a racially biased attitude against Caucasians was a major thing I abandoned. Some of the kindest people I met at Science were friends of mine who happened to be white. One girl I knew was raised in a family who couldn't stand black people and was considered an outcast because she was so disgusted with their bigotry. Dad also taught us that each gender had its own role. A male is supposed to be a strong provider who doesn't show weakness or emotion. Anything less made him a "faggot." At the same time, when an assertive female felt she could handle herself without a man's help, Dad called it a result of "Butch Propaganda." You can imagine how backwards this sounded to me, considering how our household was run. Occasionally I would go against my better judgment by engaging in a serious conversation with Dad, voicing my opinion that a person's strength and potential wasn't based on their gender. These discussions always ended badly, with him saying that I needed to reevaluate my way of thinking. Cheryl would say that I was making myself look stupid or that I needed to stop thinking I knew everything. Dad was smarter. She continued to try to convince me that members of our family secretly felt the same way and couldn't stand me.

My father and sister's attitude and unpredictable reactions towards anything I said was something I couldn't always stomach, so I generally stayed in my room alone. Some days I'd sit in bed and read or listen to music. There were many nights that I'd just lay in bed crying. During one period, Mary J. Blige's song "My Life" was on repeat for months in my CD player, as I wept and imagined living a life where I was loved. I'd cry from loneliness. I'd cry from being frustrated with a sister I loved who hated me with a passion. I'd cry in mourning of my father whom I feared would eventually die from a narcotic I'd grown to despise. I felt so powerless. I wanted to save my dad. I wanted to save my people.

Being aware that there were children being starved, tortured and mentally abused was excruciating. The violence, the hatred, and the ignorance were at a level that was deafening. Kids all around me were being killed, having babies, and falling prey to criminal behavior. Still, I tried to keep telling myself that misery couldn't be all that there was. Just hold on, Moses…

- CHAPTER 13 -

The Day I Was Born

There were a string of little triumphs during the last 18 months of my countdown to freedom, which gave me hope that I would survive the hell that had been my life. As a junior, I along with my peers had the new task of looking at potential colleges to apply to. All I really wanted was to go to a school where I could major in dance and live on campus. Somewhere in the back of my mind, I actually expected something catastrophic to happen that would disqualify me from having the privilege of a college education. I hoped I could just slip in with the crowd without being noticed. Then all of a sudden, I started receiving mail. It seemed like every college in the country was sending Bronx Science students literature and booklets to encourage us to apply to their schools. The reputation of Science students is what attracted those colleges, meaning that an average student like me had a better chance of getting in than an honor student from a low performing school. Every single day, the mailbox was packed to capacity. Dad and Cheryl didn't know what to think. I kept my composure, but inside I was excited. This was really happening.

I also started doing more shows. I was joined onstage by a few of my friends who were featured in my act while a couple served as my bodyguards. At this point I was all too familiar with being chased, having costumes ripped and getting bruises from crowds mobbing me. One of the seven shows I did over a 6-week period was at my old junior high school. I was so glad that I was able to perform for my former teachers and Shugie, but the students were going crazy that day. There were hundreds of children running after us, trying to get my autograph after the performance. My father was supposed to go to that show but he got there late. I caught sight of him briefly as he was heading into the auditorium after my performance was over, but my team was trying to get me to safety because the kids were out of control. I ended up hiding in a room with my bodyguards as the students tried to break the door down. I remember us sitting in there looking at each other, wondering why they were so hysterical. They knew I wasn't actually Michael Jackson. I never wore the make-up. I just concentrated on dancing. I was good, but I was nowhere near Michael's level. We waited inside until we were told that all the kids were dismissed, but there were over 100 of them outside waiting for me as we exited. I don't know how many autographs I signed that day. When I got home, Dad tried to downplay my performances (though he hadn't seen me perform yet), saying that all I was doing was impersonating someone else, but Cheryl was excited. She encouraged me to come outside and dance for some kids in the neighborhood, which thrilled them. I even let them touch my glove and hat. While I was talking to them, I failed to notice that a group of random people on the block had assembled around me. Amongst the crowd were quite a few thugs and drug dealers I saw every day. They wanted to see what I could do, so I danced my heart out. Those people actually applauded at the end. That was heavy. Later on that week, I got my first piece of fan mail from a kid at the show I'd done at my old school.

I did "Smooth Criminal" for the talent show at school that year. I'd gotten a white suit at a men's clothing store, though I couldn't find a white fedora. I practiced for hours in my room, but it was hard to judge what I looked like while executing the moves because I had no mirrors. I would rely on watching my shadow to get a rough idea, while hoping I was doing the choreography justice. Much of what I did was based off of memory from what I'd seen Michael do because I didn't have a machine at home to play the VHS tapes my friends would make for me. Sometimes I would find an empty room with a TV/VCR combo at school and watch the tapes during my lunch periods, but it wasn't nearly enough. I needed hours of study and practice. I'd often practice shifting my weight and sliding in the hallways right before class. During a fresh snowfall, I would moonwalk the perimeter of the entire schoolyard. I would do this while wearing my worn-out sneakers, but the snow made the ground's surface smooth enough for me to slide on. In order to get better, I needed to continue to develop the muscles in my legs.

It was nice to have a couple of my buddies on stage performing with me during that show. They weren't professional dancers, but their presence really enhanced the act. I also did a short solo at the end. I asked the lighting technicians to give me a single spotlight during this portion, positioned in a way that allowed the audience to watch me dance with my shadow as I had always done at home. When I viewed the tape of the performance later, I was pleased at how well that part turned out.

Dad showed up in time to see my performance but he didn't stick around long after. There were people crowded around me offering their congratulations when he made his way over to tell me I did well. That was the only time my father ever stepped foot inside of my high school.

When our boys' basketball team was scheduled to match up against Cheryl's school, our coach told me I could do the halftime show. When I showed up to perform, our team was losing terribly and the coach was furious. I tried to let him know that I was ready to perform, but he refused to allow it and waved me away. I was in tears. The crowd that was packed in the bleachers saw what was going on and started vocally expressing their disapproval. I'm not sure what I was thinking but I turned to them, held up my hand, and announced that I'd be performing downstairs at the Food Fair, which was being held in the cafeteria that day. I added that I'd be starting in the next five minutes and if anyone wanted to see the performance, they should follow me out of an exit I pointed to. Everyone got up and left. Even the principal left. The angry coach turned around just in time to see the bleachers emptying out. He looked at me in utter shock and I stared back with a fearless expression, which sent the opposing team into a frenzy of laughter. When they got back to school (after beating the crap out of our team), they told everyone, especially Cheryl, what I'd done. They said that the coach tried to *"diss"* me but then, *"She waved her hand like Malcolm X and everybody left!"* I laughed as Cheryl described how the boys tried to reenact the whole scene, but she thought I'd done the coolest thing in the world.

I went to summer school to make up for another math class I failed. The summer school math teacher I had that year ended up being the best educator I would have during all four years of high school. After only four weeks under Mr. Freeman's instruction, I scored a 90% on the math Regents exam, which I'd failed earlier that spring. This helped reestablish my faith in my ability to excel academically. All I needed was an educator who knew how to effectively communicate ideas.

I wasn't expecting the best thing that happened to me that summer. I was in Harlem, trying to renew my certification in standard first aid and CPR, but my appointment had been cancelled. Disappointed, I started heading back home, and as I was walking by the Apollo Theater, I noticed a sign indicating that there would be auditions for the Amateur Night show held there the following morning. I stared at the flyer and took note of the details before saying to myself, *I'm not ready.* I slowly walked away, but on the way home, those words kept shooting down all of the reasons why I wanted to go to the audition. When I finally lay down in bed later that night, I couldn't rest with my decision. *Why not give it a try? What if they like it? Maybe they'll go easy on you because you're a girl. Ha!* I had to laugh at that thought. The Apollo Theater audience was notorious for shutting down anybody who wasn't up to par. Race, age, and talent genre did not matter in those days. If you didn't know what you were doing, they wouldn't allow you to stay. They would boo you off the stage. It still sounded better than possibly being shot or jumped by the crowd of drug dealers who ended up liking my performance at the playground. Besides, if I didn't try, this probably wouldn't be the last night I'd lose sleep over it. After a few hours of going back and forth, I decided to go to the audition. Dad and Cheryl were asleep by the time I'd made up my mind, so I quietly got up and went into the kitchen to practice with my hat in the dark. I felt better after I'd worked up a little sweat. When I was done, I crept back into my room and finally fell asleep.

I headed out extra early the following morning because I didn't have any train fare to get to Harlem, so I'd have to walk. The air was still cool outside but it was only a matter of time before the summer sun began to roast everything, so I hurried. There were a few people on the line at the back-door entrance when I arrived, but the line grew considerably as time went by. Some of the people chatted with each other about their talents and how far they'd come to get to the audition, but I didn't join in the conversation. Someone finally opened the door and directed us to go inside, where we signed in and took seats in the audience. The stage was surprisingly small, but the designs on the theater walls were elegant.

The coordinator of the show came in and did a short introduction about the Apollo and what would be expected of us. Soon after, she began to call the acts up to the stage, one by one. Each person proceeded to do their act until the coordinator felt she'd seen enough. This took anywhere between 30 seconds to a minute. After this, she thanked them and they left the stage. There were pauses varying in length in-between each audition, so things moved slowly. One person was stopped within seconds because her act was sexually inappropriate. She was supposed to do stand-up comedy, but she was dressed in a bikini with a pale dildo hanging out of the side of her bikini bottom. The coordinator told her to leave the theater immediately. She advised the rest of us to tone down our act if it was anything like what we'd just seen because Amateur Night was a family show. There was another guy who was just plain terrible. He sang a hateful song with his acoustic guitar in a gruff voice. I wondered if he was part of a practical joke, but he was serious. The rest of the acts were pretty good for the most part, and we applauded each person after they finished.

I tried to stay loose by stretching a little in the back of the theater because I had no idea when my name would be called. The other potential contestants seemed to relax more as time passed. Some of them kept looking over at me and I could tell they were trying to figure out what my act was. One of them came over to me and asked what I was going to do. I just told them that I'd be dancing.

When my name was finally called, I grabbed my hat and sequined glove from my bag and approached the stage amid whispered exclamations of *"Oh Shit!"* from the other acts. After introducing myself to the lady in charge, I gave my music to the sound guy. As soon as "Billie Jean" started to play, I began to pose and dance as hard as I could. The crew and the coordinator didn't say anything, but I could feel them reacting to me as I danced. I'd been going for well over a couple of minutes when I cued them to stop my music. When I did, the place erupted into applause. Before I could exit the stage, the coordinator told me the date she wanted to schedule me to perform on, which was August 30. It was a day after Michael Jackson's birthday. I confirmed my contact information with her, thanked her and left the theater on cloud nine. I kept saying to myself, *"I'm going to be on television!"* not realizing that this was "Amateur Night" which, unlike *Showtime at the Apollo*, was not televised. Maybe my father would be proud of me as a performer if I did well at this world-famous venue. I had my fingers crossed.

It was mid-afternoon and the sun was blazing as I walked back to the Bronx. Cheryl was beyond excited when she found out that I passed the audition. Even my father was happy for me. I went to work immediately, sewing 6,500 pieces of silver sequins into a black, long-sleeve, button-down shirt I'd bought a year before. The idea was to make it look like the top Michael had worn during his *Motown 25* performance. Every day, I came home from school and worked on that shirt for hours at a time. I put the shirt on a hanger and hung it from a long, old-fashioned lamp, which Dad had found in the street years before. It was as hot as ever in the apartment that summer and working under that lamp didn't help matters, but I wanted to sew the shirt properly. There would be sweat pouring off me as I worked, but my concentration was too heavy to warrant any complaint from me. It took a month to complete the shirt and I used the rest of the sequins to make a pair of socks.

During the weeks leading up to the show, I'd invited as many people as I could. Dad said he'd definitely be there, and if Cheryl had the money to pay for commercial advertisements, I think she would have. She told *everybody*. It's still a mystery to me how the animosity she had towards me turned off completely when I had to perform. Back then she was my biggest fan.

During practice on the day of the show, I made a careless mistake that could have kept me from performing that night. After doing a spin, I dropped to my knees, as I'd seen Michael Jackson and James Brown do. The problem was that I was on concrete and I wasn't wearing any kneepads. This did not incapacitate me but it damn sure didn't tickle, my right knee in particular. Fortunately, I wasn't injured bad enough to cancel the show. I took my time packing and rested until it was time for me to go to the sound check. On my way out, Dad told me he probably wouldn't make it but that I should try to enjoy myself onstage. I thanked him for wishing me well and left. There was no time to worry about not having him there, though I really wished he hadn't told me this. I would have felt better performing under the assumption that he was there, even if he didn't show up. There was a crowd of 1,500 judges I had to battle that night. I needed to focus.

One of my bodyguards, Natalion Seymour, whom I called "Apache," met me at the theater. The other contestants were inside the theater waiting to start the sound check, when we arrived. They all made friendly conversation with each other, but it was obvious that they were making note of who amongst us were the strongest performers. Apparently, some of the people doing sound checks were scheduled to perform on a later date. A few contestants kept asking performers who'd completed their sound checks if they were in the show that night. I had no clue about all of this, but it didn't matter to me anyway. The only performer I had to worry about was myself. After my sound check, a few contestants asked if I was going to perform that night and looked very disappointed when I gave my answer. After I got my dressing room assignment, Apache lead me upstairs to change. Luckily, I had a room to myself. I'm not sure if this was because I was the only minor performing that night, but it didn't bother me. Watching the other contestants size each other up wasn't a very unifying display of showmanship. I needed privacy to think, get dressed and pray. Apache stood guard outside of my door until I was ready. We prayed together then went downstairs to join the others.

The lineup of the show included a total of 22 contestants, meaning this was going to be a long night. Much to my surprise, I was scheduled to open the show. I decided that I would work extra hard to make sure the audience wouldn't forget me. The show was running late, but this was a good thing because I wasn't sure if all the people I'd invited were there yet. I knew Cheryl was out there, and possibly my younger cousin, Gina. Aunt Eunice couldn't make it but she sent her blessings. A few of my friends from school promised that they would attend. After waiting for what seemed like a month, the show started. A mixture of adrenaline and nervousness caused an indescribable feeling to go through my entire body. I was really about to do this.

I spotted Apache as he took his place, standing guard at the other end of the stage. It was time. When the host said my name, I took a breath, locked in my focus and walked out onto the stage to rub the Tree of Hope. My costume shimmered as the stage lights hit it, and the audience gave me a decent round of applause, though I could hear a few isolated boos from the front row. I didn't panic as I thought to myself, *Go ahead and boo. You're gonna be screaming like a 10-year-old girl in a few seconds.* That's exactly what went through my head at that moment. I walked over to the host, who draped a protective arm around me before asking me where I was from and what I planned to do that night. Speaking clearly into the microphone he offered, I said that I was from Harlem and that I was going to dance. He wished me well and I took my place at the center of the stage. When the music started, I went to work immediately. The audience started going crazy, but my concentration was still dominating me. There was no time to relax. This audience would turn on me in a heartbeat if I made one wrong move. I pushed myself hard and by the time the song was over, the audience was on its feet applauding. That was pure magic. Michael had been on that stage. So had James, Gladys and so many other legendary entertainers who'd contributed to the Apollo Legacy. Getting such a great response from this audience meant more to me than any other audience I'd performed for. They demanded excellence. The hard part was over. The contestants greeted me with a nice round of applause as I re-entered the green room. They peppered me with questions, asking about the crowd and how many people were out there. I told them not to get shook by the handful of haters in the front row. The next act went up soon after and the show fell into a rhythm. There were some close calls and a couple of people got booed off. I tried to console these contestants, some of which were crying, telling them not to quit. James Brown got booed at the Apollo before he hit big. Sandman Sims wasn't present to throw acts off of the stage after they got booed. In his place was CP Lacey, the Michael Jackson impersonator I'd seen years before in junior high school. At the Apollo, he was known as The Executioner. He came over to tell me how much he enjoyed my performance. Getting a compliment like that from CP was a big deal for me.

After the last act, all of the remaining contestants lined up to walk out for the judging. I could already hear the audience screaming, "Michael!" We went out in the order that we'd performed in, putting me at the head of the line. As soon as the audience spotted me on stage, they started cheering. I looked for Cheryl, but the lights were so bright that it was almost impossible to make out anyone's face in the audience. The crowd was cheering so loud that there was no way I could have even detected the direction from which her voice might be coming from. By the time we were all lined up on stage, the crowd was still going strong and the host had to quiet them down. The spokesmodel whose job it was to present each act came over to me first. The audience stood up and poured their hearts out. I was so astounded by their waves of energy that I thought I was going to fall over. *All of this, for me?* I thought. I bowed, thanked them and stepped back into the line, but they weren't done. They started chanting, *"Michael! Michael..."* even as the spokesmodel had moved on to the next contestant. Not knowing what to do, the host looked to the coordinator of the show, who was in the wings. She signaled him to announce me as the first place winner so that the judging for second and third place could proceed. When he did, the audience gave me another beautiful standing ovation. There I was, a poor, ugly, 17-year-old ghetto child being treated like royalty on one of the greatest stages in the world. My first reaction to this opportunity had been wrong. I *was* ready.

I received many congratulations from the other performers, as we were getting ready to leave that night. Apache went downstairs to check the crowd while I packed up to leave. When he returned, he said, "This is gonna be bad." According to him, there was a large crowd waiting for me at the back door. He said the front exit was worse, so we decided to take the rear exit. He led me downstairs and shielded me as they opened the back door. The crowd outside was so packed that we couldn't just walk out. Cheryl and a few of my friends were amongst the crowd, giving me hugs and telling me what a great job I'd done. I signed autographs and shook hands with other spectators, thanking them as they congratulated me. They fired questions at me and a few people gave me their contact information because they wanted to book me for shows. Cheryl and my friends helped walk me through the crowd, but people kept stopping me. Cheryl let me know that Gina had been in the audience, but she left because the show ran too long. However, not much could bother me at that moment. For the first time in many years, I was overwhelmed with joy.

Once school started again, I invited my friends to the three additional Amateur Night shows that I was in. The school newspaper even did an article about my performances. I placed second and third in 2 of the shows, but I didn't win the "Super Top Dog." The coordinator of the show actually sounded "The Executioner" alarm on me that night to get me off the stage because my performance ran too long. Doug E. Fresh was hosting that night and he hyped up the crowd to get me entered into the judging at the end. I made it to the top four but I didn't win. I wasn't heartbroken because I had proven to myself that I could perform on any stage in the world if I really wanted to.

That November I applied to four colleges, including SUNY Potsdam. I had my eye on that school because I could enter as a dance major without an audition. Senior year was a breeze because I'd taken care of all my major requirements during my junior year overload. I fell asleep twice during my SATs and scored an 1110. Damn, I wish I'd stayed awake. Cheryl seemed to sense that my time at home was drawing to an end. She and I were able to talk more often without her being cross with me. I'd more or less figured out how to stay out of my father's way and catch him for a chat when he was in a good mood. I really wished that I could save him. Sometimes I'd catch an oldies station playing songs he hadn't heard in years and I'd record them for him. Surprisingly enough, the artists whose music I'd become most familiar with at this point (besides Michael Jackson) were The Beatles. John Lennon was a master at melody writing and his lyrics were profound. I had written about twenty songs by then and was outlining stories that would later become scripts. I couldn't afford Michael's latest album, *HIStory*, but a friend of mine let me borrow hers and I recorded it on cassettes. That album was powerful. Somehow I convinced my father to listen to "Stranger in Moscow" which he loved, though his all-time favorite MJ song was "Dirty Diana." "Earth Song" was strong enough to bring tears to my eyes. When the video came out, I didn't know what to think. That man was good. Getting my father to open up to the music that inspired me felt like I had a prayer in getting through to him one day. If you can understand the music in a person's heart, you can understand the person. Music stayed with me all day. There was always a song stuck in my head, giving rhythm to my stride or my workflow, as well as singing me to sleep if I had the blues.

The last half of senior year was nothing but fun. The workload was moderate, there were all kinds of silly dress-up days at school, and the overall atmosphere was so stress-free. Shugie was expecting her first child, which was exciting news. Cheryl and I would visit her at her school and make sure that her rowdy students knew not to mess with her, though she handled herself better than most of the teachers there.

There was a snowstorm that shut down the schools for a couple of days. The Bronx had never looked so pretty to me. Cheryl had dropped out of school by this time and I was free to hang out with her that day. We literally spent the day playing in the snow.

I was ecstatic when I got into SUNY Potsdam as a dance major. It was so far upstate that a 20-minute drive would lead you into Canada. I'd be living on campus with the option to work at the college during the summers instead of having to come back home. I stayed on top of my paperwork to make sure that there was no way that I would miss my chance to go away to school.

I opened my last talent show at Bronx Science with our principal, Stanley Blumenstein. We dressed up like hip-hop artists and performed a rap song we wrote. The mere sight of Stan on stage rapping had the students going nuts. He was such a great guy. In closing the show, I was joined by four very talented dancers from our school in doing Michael Jackson's "Scream." The girl who portrayed Janet, Melanie Farrah, broke her foot on stage, but she finished the performance. That girl had a lot of heart. One of my closest friends, Hallie Barrows, volunteered to emulate a crazed MJ fan that had to be carried off the stage. It was a last-minute detail that we wanted to put in, and it worked out well.

Another noteworthy highlight of senior year was when I convinced Cheryl to spend the day at school with me on my 18th birthday. Ever since she'd dropped out, I kept trying to encourage her to get her GED or go finish school. I wanted her to see that there was possibility beyond Patterson Projects and ghetto life if she would stop being angry all the time and open her mind. It was on this day that I let my guard down, and it allowed her to get a glimpse of the person I'd grown into. As soon as we stepped into the school that morning, people were greeting me with hugs, presents, and birthday cards. I got two birthday cakes, and my supervisor, Marty Jacobson, gave me the Bronx Science hoodie that I was always drooling over but couldn't afford. I still have it. Marc Marie gave me the *HIStory* album that she'd loaned me months before. Apparently, she was planning to give it to me for my birthday but didn't want me to have to wait to hear Michael's new music, so she let me "borrow" it as soon as it came out. Cheryl helped me carry all of my gifts as I took her to my classes where my teachers and friends welcomed her. By the end of the day, Cheryl was speechless. She said she felt like she'd never known me during our whole life together. The truth is, she'd never truly cared to listen. More than anything, I wanted this visit to inspire her to stop thinking that the struggle we'd experienced was all that the world was about.

I still had to do some work on myself though. I had to keep the promise I'd made to be active in developing my own character and erase my own ignorance, so that I could grow into the person I wanted to be. I was still in the closet, so that GOD wouldn't be mad at me, but even that concept was ceasing to add up. If GOD doesn't approve of lies, what made it okay for me to lie about who

I was? I didn't make myself this way, and it certainly wasn't taught to me. I was not ready to come out yet, but at least I was trying to come to terms with this issue. Besides, if Michael Jackson ever got within 20 feet of me, there would be no need for me to come out of the closet.

I almost missed the senior trip because I thought it was on a later date. It wasn't until I got to school on the morning of the trip that I figured out my mistake. I told my friends that I couldn't go because I was broke until the next day. I remember Melanie Farrah telling me that they were not going to leave until I got my ass on that bus. Before I knew it, I was on a bus heading to Six Flags in New Jersey. My friends treated me to anything I wanted and practically held my hand during my first time on a roller coaster. It may have seemed like no big deal to them, but the kindness they displayed left me in tears that day.

My cousin Rhonda Windham, Shugie's older sister, paid for my senior pictures and Officer Robinson treated me to a trip to a beautician to get my hair done for the prom. I went with one of my friends because the guy I wanted to ask had a girlfriend. Even if I were out of the closet, there was only one girl in all my years in high school who I was attracted to. I would have been too shy to ask her anyway. To tell the truth, I wasn't really attracted to any of my peers until senior year. Up until then, they all looked like kids to me.

There was also an awards ceremony held at our school, and I took home the award for best entertainer of the senior class. To my surprise, there was a check for over $700 that came along with the award. That was a pure blessing. GOD made a way for me to be able to pay for supplies I would need once I got to school. Shugie was at the ceremony and agreed to deposit it into her checking account, which she gave me little by little when it cleared. We kept this a secret because if my father found out, he'd want his cut and raise hell if I refused to give him any of it. I also didn't want to lie to him if he asked me for money to get high in the middle of the night. If the money was in Shugie's account, I could tell him I didn't have any cash without actually lying to him.

I was scheduled to perform at my graduation, which was held at Madison Square Garden, along with three of my friends who were amazing dancers. I designed the piece to show how any true dancer could appreciate the different forms of dance outside of their genre. The first person would perform ballet until the music changed, causing the next person to invade the stage, dancing as a warrior to African drums. The two would collaborate and after a minute or so, the music would switch to hip-hop and the next dancer would take the stage. The three of them would join in together until "Billie Jean" came on and I moonwalked on the stage. The dance concluded with the four of us performing a little combination of moves taken from each style.

I was home getting ready on the day of graduation, when Cheryl came in the room and said that my father was telling her that he didn't want to go. He told her that he didn't want to embarrass me in front of my friends because he looked like a crack-head. She said this was why he never went to any of my shows. He thought he was too low to be around me.

I didn't have time to find out why the HELL she hadn't told this to me years ago, but I had no intentions of putting up with his issues on that day. Dad and Cheryl had attended all of my graduations since elementary school. This was not about to change. This was *my* day. I walked into his room and before I could speak, he started explaining in a nonchalant way that he might have to miss my graduation. I let him talk as a grin slowly grew into a wide smile on my face until I actually started giggling. He chuckled a bit too, confused, as he interrupted his own little speech, asking what was so funny. Without taking my eyes off of him, I responded, "He's so cute, he thinks he gets a vote." He was silent as my face became serious and I continued, "You're going. You don't get a vote." I'd never ordered my father to do anything but I wasn't in a negotiating mood. He had tears in his eyes as he responded by picking out a shirt to wear, combing his hair and washing his face. Soon after, the three of us headed to Madison Square Garden.

What I remember most about graduation day was our performance, which was the highlight if you ask me. I was in tears, watching from the wings as each of the dancers performed and acted out the scenes I'd given them. By the time I moonwalked onto the stage to join them, I felt like I'd already made my point. If artists from different genres could celebrate and collaborate with each other, a peaceful coexistence between people of different colors, backgrounds and religions could be accomplished on Earth. That was the most valuable lesson I learned at Bronx High School of Science.

The summer of '96 was pretty quiet. My father and I didn't speak much, but Cheryl spent almost every day with me. We didn't really argue and she even fell asleep in my bed on some nights. Her wanting to be around me was strange because she'd never treated me like that before. I kept trying to encourage her to get something going before I left. I warned her that when I went away to school, Dad's drug problem was likely to become more apparent. We both knew that my presence was a reminder to him that he could do better for himself and that he needed to do something to treat his addiction. Cheryl did end up getting her GED, but she wasn't working and this worried me. I didn't want her to be stuck in there with no money, having to turn a blind eye to my father's issue. She had a bad habit of going into spouts of denial about his problem because she thought that addressing it was a form of betrayal. I didn't want to fight with her about it, but I wished desperately that she would open her eyes.

SUNY Potsdam sent my dorm assignment, but I'm convinced that GOD HIM/HERSELF chose the date that I was required to report to campus—August 29, 1996. That was Michael Jackson's 38th birthday. As the summer dragged on, I slowly used the money from my award to purchase clothes, toiletries and supplies I'd need for school. By August 28, I literally had 25 cents left in my pocket. Shugie had promised that she wouldn't let me go to school without any cash, but I couldn't get her on the phone that day. I found out why soon enough. She'd given birth to her son, Brandyn. Cheryl and I rushed to the hospital immediately to see her. I was particularly happy because Brandyn was supposed to be born the following week. If he'd been born on schedule, I wouldn't have gotten a chance to meet him until winter break. He was beautiful. He looked just like Shugie. I couldn't stay long because I had to figure out how I was going to get to school the next day, but Shugie worked her magic again. Her friend, Kajana Stevens, would drive me to the bus station. Before I left the hospital, Shugie handed me $70. She was still lying in the bed she'd given birth to her son in. GOD bless that woman.

I got home that night, finished packing and called the bus station to find out what time my bus would be leaving. When Dad came home, the tension in the house grew. We'd hardly spoken all summer and now that I was leaving in the morning, he finally opened his mouth. He was clearly aggravated as he said that the reason why he hadn't spoken much to me about leaving for college was because I'd left him years ago. He picked the wrong day to go there with me. I told him that we didn't leave him, at which he failed at an attempt to interrupt me as I shouted over him, "You left us for that white woman!" ("White Woman" is street slang for cocaine.) He shut up. We both knew that there was too much for us to say to each other and no time to say it, so we left it at that.

The following morning, Kajana Stevens and my cousin Chandler (Shugie's little brother) showed up, and we began to pack my belongings into her car. I took my stereo, tapes, CDs and all my clothes. The walls where my MJ posters had been were now bare. I didn't realize how much my belongings livened up our room until I'd moved them out.

Toni Braxton's song, "Let It Flow," was on repeat in my head that morning. The lyrics were about not being afraid to choose freedom over a painful chapter in your life. I still feel like she sang that song just for me on that day. As I was about to walk out of my room for the last time, Cheryl came out of nowhere and hugged me as she started sobbing in my arms. She started apologizing for always being so mean to me, but I told her not to worry and that I'd call her when I got to my dorm. My father was a little teary-eyed and didn't say much, I suspect, because he was afraid to break down in front of me. I hugged him, told him I loved him and walked outside to go to the car. As we pulled off, I could see him standing in front of the building watching. As we drove off the block, I quietly vowed that I would never spend another night in that apartment again.

My motion sickness was acting up as we headed to the bus station, although Chandler thought it was anxiety. He couldn't have been more wrong. I was the last person to board the bus heading to Potsdam, New York, but I made it. After Chandler put the remaining pieces of my luggage into the compartment under the bus, the doors slammed closed and the bus slowly pulled off.

It was in that moment that the chains that had kept me bound to misery were finally lifted and I haven't seen them since.

ABOUT THE AUTHOR

Moses Harper earned a Bachelor's degree in Music from SUNY Purchase in 2001. Since then, she's become a performing artist, writer, mentor and motivational speaker. She's made appearances on *The Today Show, 106 & Park* and is a lead choreographer and outreach coordinator with *Thrill the World NYC*, a non-profit organization that celebrates Michael Jackson's legacy through performance and donating to charities all over the world. In 2011 she was the winner of the Amateur Night Super Top Dog competition at the Apollo Theater, where she has performed as a Michael Jackson tribute artist 20 times. Her work with high-risk youth inspired her to develop and implement an original curriculum designed to encourage young people to be empowered in life. She's currently producing her first film and completing a second book.

For more information, visit her at www.mosesharper.com

www.ingramcontent.com/pod-product-compliance
Lightning Source LLC
LaVergne TN
LVHW011156080426
835508LV00007B/440